Mr. Right,
Right
Now!

THE
MAN CATCHING
METHOD
THAT
DROPS CHAPS
IN THEIR
TRACKS!

How a Smart Woman Can Land Her Dream Man in **6** **WEEKS**

Mr. Right, Right Now!

By

Jean E. Carroll

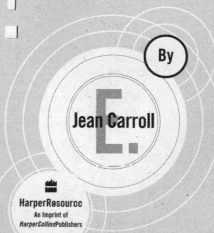

HarperResource

An Imprint of
*HarperCollins*Publishers

MR. RIGHT, RIGHT NOW! MAN CATCHING MADE EASY. *Copyright © by E. Jean Carroll. All rights reserved in the Northern Hemisphere, the Southern Hemisphere, the earth, the solar system, the universe, which, come to think of it, is probably merely the creation of a superior race of women on* another *planet, in* another *solar system, in* another *universe, so I would like to reserve rights on* that *planet, in* that *solar system, and* that *universe too.*

MR. RIGHT, RIGHT NOW! Copyright © 2004, 2005 by E. Jean Carroll. All rights reserved. Printed in the United States of America. No part of this book may be used or reproduced in any manner whatsoever without written permission except in the case of brief quotations embodied in critical articles and reviews. For information, address HarperCollins Publishers Inc., 10 East 53rd Street, New York, NY 10022.

HarperCollins books may be purchased for educational, business, or sales promotional use. For information, please write: Special Markets Department, HarperCollins Publishers Inc., 10 East 53rd Street, New York, NY 10022.

First HarperResource paperback edition published 2005

Design by Judith Stagnitto Abbate/Abbate Design

Library of Congress Cataloging-in-Publication Data is available upon request.

ISBN 0-06-053029-4 (pbk.)

05 06 07 08 09 WBC/RRD 10 9 8 7 6 5 4 3 2 1

Any resemblance to an actual living person is intended, and that actual person is you, Doll; and you're going to start living Right Now!

The final aim of all love intrigues, be they comic or tragic, is really of more importance than all other ends in human life. What it all turns upon is nothing less than the composition of the next generation. It's not the weal and woe of any one individual, but that of the human race to come, which is here at stake.

Arthur Schopenhauer

Back up, boy, I ain't your toy.

Missy Elliott

Contents

Acknowledgments

1. Dolls, the author acknowledges there are too many self-help books

2. The author acknowledges the main reason there are too many self-help books is that self-help-book authors raise hopes to such ridiculously high levels by presenting such diabolically alluring success stories, the poor reader feels worse than before he/she bought the self-help book. The reader, being a mere human and a lovable chucklehead, is of course incapable of achieving such success, so the reader must buy another self-help book to pep him/herself up after the hellish depression he/she suffered from reading the last self-help book, and so on.

3. The author wishes to acknowledge this book is written for smart, successful women and that these women are just way smarter and more successful than the author.

4. The author also wishes to acknowledge there's going to be a problem with Mr. Right, Right Now! because the 6-Week Plan

*is so wickedly effective at bagging men, in two years the au-
thor will be flooded with letters from women beseeching the author to tell them how to get rid of the fellows they landed by
following it.*

5. *The author is just dying to acknowledge this book was initially
subtitled* How a Smart Woman Can Land Her Dream Man in
10 Weeks.

6. *But then the author and the author's sister accidentally started
GreatBoyfriends.com, an Internet dating site, and* The New
York Times *and* The Today Show *and* Oprah *made a big
whoop-dee-doo over it and thousands of women signed up and
men began crashing into their arms like felled timbers.*

7. *This stunned the author, so the author began conducting major forehead-slapping interviews with bleeding-edge Harvard
psychologists, Rutgers anthropologists, and Oxford evolutionary biologists and learned about "clicking" and "rapid attraction systems" and "inborn courting behavior" and discovered
that 10 weeks was just insanely wide of the mark. So the author changed the subtitle to* How a Smart Woman Can Land
Her Dream Man in **6** Weeks, *which, indeed, the author wishes
to acknowledge is still pretty long, because if a woman meets
the right man, it takes about six seconds to land the bugger.*

Introduction

Genesis of the Man Catching Theory

Whoa, now. You are about to start reading *Mr. Right, Right Now!—How a Smart Woman Can Land Her Dream Man in 6 Weeks.* How exciting. You are whomp-whomping through the pages, eager to get to the Man Catching Theory. Excellent! You are now faced with a quandary:

Should you read the Introduction? Or skip it? Frankly even the author finds the Introduction a tad long and technical. The major themes it tackles are:

A. *How all theories should be tested.*

B. *How it would be difficult to test the Man Catching Theory without tracking huge numbers of men and women.*

C. *How the aforementioned GreatBoyfriends.com is started by the author and the author's sister Cande.*

D. *How the author is surprised by the millions of hits on GreatBoyfriends.com.*

E. *How the author goes out on the town to celebrate with pineapple martinis the millions of hits.*

F. *How she wakes up the next day feeling like a four-inch Manolo Blahnik heel (the open-toed, white patent-leather from three years ago) is wedged in her forehead.*

G. *How she turns on her iMac, and despite being hungover, how she looks at the screen and suddenly realizes that for the first time in human history, thanks to the dazzling flow of Internet code, that* mystery of mysteries—*how women catch men*—*is being revealed to her.*

H. *How the bursts of zeros and ones make it stupendously clear to the author that (1) her Man Catching Theory <u>is</u> being tested and that (2) the Man Catching Method drops chaps in their tracks.*

I. *How she decides to always capitalize the "M" and the "C" in Man Catching and chuck the hyphen.*

J. *How the hard evidence gathered from thousands of letters sent to the* Ask E. Jean *column at the fabled* Elle *magazine supports the massive data from GreatBoyfriends.com and bolsters the basic premise of the Man Catching Theory.*

K. *How no theory is ever complete, but how if any of those other so-called "love advice" books like* The Rules *actually worked, everybody would already <u>be</u> married.*

L. *How if you've read this far and think this part should also be skipped, it is already too late.*

Part One

Bring me that tall, handsome young officer of the Imperial Horse Guard!

Catherine the Great

Bum chicky, chick bum
Shake ya **bum bum**

Lil' Kim

3 Simple Reasons the Man Catching Theory Will Work for You in **6** Weeks . . . or Less

Reason #1

Honey, You Were *Born* to Drive Men Mad

Mr. Right, Right Now!'s Man Catching Theory (which works so well, it will one day have hair gels, breath mints, and contraceptives named after it) is rooted in the fact that you are already fitted-out by nature to find and seduce a man. You are so designed because Mom Nature wants you out there rollicking and creating new combinations of genes, and Mom gets her new gene-combinations only if men are pestering you for sex in their $3.7-million penthouses.

Don't Believe You're Fitted-Out by Nature to
Seduce a Man?

P-shaw!

Let me ask you one question: Have men gone to extravagant lengths over the last 30,000 years to *control* females' seductiveness with chastity belts, clitoridectomies, foot bindings, veils, purdahs, stonings, the rules of three Big Religions, etc., etc., etc.?

Come on, honey . . .

Let me ask you another question: Would chaps around the world, in nearly every country, put this much effort into controlling your attractions if you weren't just unbelievably, incredibly *hot*?

The *Mr. Right, Right Now!* **6-Week Plan** is going to *build* on this fact.

And What Are These Natural Attractors That
Drive the Poor Buggers Insane?

They are the same from the Hamptons to the highlands of New Guinea. Women are composed of 100 billion neurons, and when they see a chap they like, the suckers start firing with the express purpose of torturing him. (Evolutionary biologists and anthropologists refer to this torture as "sending signals.")

These signals consist of smiling at a man, looking away, gazing back at him from under your lashes, ignoring him, glancing at him again, giving off an alluring scent, displaying more curves than the

Ventura Freeway, walking with an animated fanny, and so on. All these provocative attention-getters help cause the right man to drop in your tracks like a bug on a flystrip.

Needless to say, the *Mr. Right, Right Now!* **6-Week Plan** did not get off the boat with a shawl on its head and will build on these signals.

And Whence Did Your Animated Fanny Spring?

Why, nothing could be simpler. You inherited your ability to find and seduce a man from your foremothers. Let's put it this way: If every single one of your foremothers had not found and seduced a man, you would not be here reading that every single one of your foremothers found and seduced a man. Perhaps this little Time Table will illustrate:

The History of Your Sex Appeal

From the Beginning of the World to the Present Moment

4,000,000,000 B.C. . . .

A bunch of carbon and stuff is swirling around which is not really very interesting, so let's move on to . . .

3,800,000,000 B.C. . . .

Your first foremother appears. She is a heterotroph, which vaguely resembles Diane Sawyer's nose/a modern bacterium, depending on your perspective. Trust me on this.

3,799,999,999 B.C. . . .

Your foremama exchanges "genetic information" with another heterotroph and is credited with enjoying the world's first snog.

2,862,997,329 B.C. . . .

Other cells and shapely organisms join your foremother in a *Boogie Nights*–type orgy, and snogging becomes contagious—literally. (The case can be made that you carry thi "infectious" snogging element your DNA, and if I knew anything at all about it, I'd ma the case myself.)

Okay, the next few billion years nothing much is going on except some Chuck Darwin–type events with your sponges, your worms, your mollusks, your jellyfish, your brontosauri, and, of course, your mammals, who start up with their humping and their yowling and their scratching and their you-drive-me-half-insane-with-passion snogging as if the future of the world depended on it . . .

7,000,000 B.C. . . .

Your foremothers make their debuts as hominids—ancestresses of apes and humans with the jaws of Joan Crawford—and spend their days copulating just all the damn time, like *dozens* of times a day. Yes, Doll, I can say, without exaggeration, there is never a single sperm swimming free *anywhere* in the vicinity of your foremothers, if they can help it.

1,600,000 B.C. . . .

Your *Homo erectus* foremothers are not *quite* the total sluts as your hominids (though they certainly enjoy a little tickle-me-pickle-me whenever they can get it). The fact remains: if over the previous 6 million years your foremothers had *not* evolved attraction skills . . . if they had *not* adapted all kinds of bewitching torments to lure your forefathers into boffing and reproducing, as I mentioned before, *you* would not be here.

30,000 B.C. . . .

Your modern foremothers take over. But since a lot of tedious events occur after this date, like the invention of the chastity belt and the debut of the Dr. Phil show—and since the only reason I have for writing this Time Line is to prove that you come from an *extremely* long line of off-the-charts-captivating forebabes—*not one of whom failed in attracting at least one mate*—which I flatter myself with having brilliantly accomplished, I shall now state the one date that I'm completely certain of: today is June 29, 2003.

Feeling more confident? Good. The *Mr. Right, Right Now!*
6-Week Plan is going to build on your confidence. And for an extra little boost, listen to what the famous Rutgers anthropologist and
ethologist (a scientist who's interested in the genetic aspects of behavior) Dr. Helen Fisher told me. Not only does she believe the per-
sistence of the opening "courtship pattern" (the gazing, the grinning,
the pupil-dilating, the blushing, the breathing, the omigod-omigod-
omigod-omigod-omigod speechless thing you naturally do when
you meet a man you like) is "inborn," her research has led her to
conclude:

"We evolved the ability to fall in love at first sight from all sorts
of other creatures. All mammals feel attraction. For example," says
Dr. Fisher, "at the beginning of the breeding season a female squirrel must find herself a male squirrel. She can't spend three months
looking around. She's got to find one with a rich, furry tail and nice
whiskers, and she's got to do it *now*. So the attraction system evolved
to be triggered *very* rapidly in the brain. And I think we inherited
this system from other mammals and from our ancestors. Which
means you can walk into a crowded party tonight, see somebody
across the room, exchange a few sentences, and fall in love."

And that brings us to the second reason that the Man Catching
Theory is going to work for you in **6** weeks, or less:

Reason #2

Men Decide Pretty Much Everything About You in the First 30 Seconds

(And you can be *brilliant* for 30 seconds, right, Doll?)

Well, that's an exaggeration. It takes less than two seconds for men to suck in every detail of your hair, your clothes, your shape, your style, your status, your walk—and be driven mad with astonishment.

(And you are checking men out even more quickly. According to the evolutionary psychologist Dr. Geoffrey Miller, a human female can judge the "physical attractiveness" of a male face in one-seventh of a second. Yours truly judges Dr. Geoffrey Miller to be a handsome specimen from a one-seventh glance at his author photo on his book.)

Men absolutely lose their brains over novelty and beauty. And even if a man simply "likes" the way you look, or is "mildly provoked" by the way you look—everything *after* that is fixed by his first impression.

"The impression is anchored," says Dr. Frank Bernieri, the Harvard Ph.D., associate professor at Oregon State University, and the world's leading expert on the subject.[1]

"We *feel* these other bits of information are revealed to us independently, but no," says Dr. Bernieri. "They are absolutely an-

---

1. Really, this instant-love stuff is all as old as Homer. It's Romeo and Juliet. It's Anna and Vronksy. It's Tramp and Lady. It's Michael Corleone in *The Godfather* looking at Appollonia just once on that hot Sicilian hillside, high-tailing it back to the village and asking for her hand in marriage.

chored by that first sight. When a guy sees an attractive woman, he *wants* to find her interesting. He *wants* to discover she's intelligent."

In fact, when a man first makes your acquaintance, the information he picks up after the initial ten or twelve seconds is *not* added on to. "People *think* they're learning more, that their judgments are better," says Dr. Bernieri, "that they're catching the nuances, but that's not the case. They're interpreting information consistent with what they *already* believe from the first few seconds. And they'll go out of their way to look for information that confirms it."

So, Doll, it's pretty much over by the time your fingertips meet his in the handshake.

Needless to say, the *Mr. Right, Right Now!* **6-Week Plan** is not going to sit on its beautiful buttocks when it comes to manipulating (in the best sense of the word!) this primal talent in men (and women) to take supremely quick first impressions.

Which brings us to the third reason the Man Catching Theory is going to help you land your dream man in 6 weeks or less:

Reason #3

When You Meet a Man, and You Like Each Other, You Will Synchronize

This is called "clicking."

"It's *amazing*!" says Dr. Bernieri, who's filmed synchrony in dozens of experiments. (Synchrony occurs when two strangers meet; they like one another; and they begin mirroring each other's movements.) "Anytime you synchronize with someone, it's *energizing*," says Dr. Bernieri. "And that's a powerful reinforcer. And when it happens, I don't care *who* you're interacting with, you can't wait for the next time you see him, because you just *love* this person!"

Dr. Bernieri has also found that if two people meet and *don't* synchronize in the first 30 seconds, chances are high, they'll *never* synchronize. What's more, you can't fake synchrony. (So-called "love coaches" have used Dr. Bernieri's research and tried to "teach" synchronizing to hapless suckers in dating courses. It never works. Good feelings cause synchrony. Faking synchrony doesn't cause good feelings.)

So what does this mean for the *Mr. Right, Right Now!* **6-Week Plan?**

It means you simply have to be yourself. Repeat. BE YOUR-SELF. It means that (A) if a fellow's crazy for you in the first ten seconds, chances are good he'll be crazy for you in the next ten seconds, and (B) if he's crazy for you and you're mad for him in the next ten seconds, you'll be nuts for each other in the *next* ten seconds, and so (C) you'll click and start synchronizing, and if you start synchronizing, then (D) you'll both be wild to see each other again, whereupon (E) if you're wild to see each other again, chances are very very good that you'll (F) synchronize the next time you're together, and if you synchronize the next time you're together, you'll synchronize the *next* time, and so on.

It means you don't have to overthink and worry and pour your brain through a sieve and get all freaked-out about what to say or how to act, because Ma Nature is taking care of nearly everything.

If there's a mantra (and why not?) of *M.R.R.N.* it is this:

Be yourself, *Ma is taking care of everything.*

Of course, you must acquire the right attitude (Week One), look devastating (Week Two), get rid of your fears (Week Three), and place yourself where there are tons of elite men (Week Four), and then . . .

"So, Doctor, *is* there love at first sight?"

Silence.

"Uhhhhhhh . . . ," says Dr. Bernieri.

Laughter.

"Maybe," says Dr. Bernieri.

Laughter.

"Listen to the Harvard Ph.D.," I say. "You big scaredy-cat."

"[Stammering] I'm counting on it."

"Really? You're *counting* on love at first sight? Has it ever happened to you, Doctor?"

Pause.

Dr. Bernieri is dating.

"I believe in love at first *minute,*" says Dr. Bernieri correcting himself.

"Aha. Why?"

"Because of the synchrony research. If you look at the tapes, they'll blow you away. People look like they're dancing. And here's a fact: when we looked at synchrony over time, what we find is that synchrony *never increases.*"

"Get out!"

"You either have it *immediately,* or you don't."

"Getthefluckouttahere!"

"And when you have it, you can lose it, anybody who's gone through a breakup knows you can lose it, but you don't ever seem to *gain* it. Or create it. So that tells me—now I'll make a leap. You meet somebody and in thirty seconds there's a click. That's how it's described—'a click'—and that clicking means you're synchroniz-

ing. You become less self-conscious. More interested. More engaged. More *exhilarated.* Time speeds up. And *that* feeling I'd call
love. If you want to say that's love at first sight, then I'll say, yep,
that'll happen in the first minute."

The Snow White Effect

So I'm calling this love-at-first-minute thing the Snow White Effect. I
was going to call it the Man Catching Effect, but that larky lass
doesn't have to do one damn thing except eat a poison apple and
bivouac in a glass coffin till a Prince rides by, and BOOM.[2] So the
Snow White Effect it is. One glance and that princely chap's swearing
400 oaths he loves Snow like no man has ever loved and is begging
the seven dwarfs to give *him* the coffin, and his vassals do the whole
Princess-Di-coffin-on-the-shoulder thing, and off they march left,
right, left, right, left, right, till they cover a distance of about eight
yards and one of them stumbles. The coffin is jolted and the apple
core, which is stuck in Snow's throat, flies out like she's been Heim-
liched by Big Mama Cass.

"Oh!" she cries.

That's an exact quote.

"Where am I?"

She tips back the lid, sits up, looks into the Prince's eyes,
and . . .

---

2. This is the Love-at-First-Sight Brothers Grimm version, not the Disney, where
the Prince first spies S. White sweeping and singing "Some Day My Prince Will
Come."

"Where are you?" says the Prince.
"You're with me, Doll.
Come to my father's castle and be my wife."

That a fairy tale can be *true*—that it can happen to you—is deliciously unnerving, to say the least. Sigmund, the Cigar Smoker, believed fairy tales were an expression of the sexual forces of our personality.

Social psychologists like Dr. Bernieri theorize that your Snow Whiting skill is prerational, developed before humans possessed language. Back in your foremama's days when she was toasting gazelle balls around the fire, she didn't know a lot of words, so all she had to go on was the way people looked. After all, she couldn't mate with *all* the fellows.

You need this zippy, instantaneous character-reading talent so you don't end up trusting just anybody who happens to come sidling along—not to mention, it can be marvelously handy at 1:30 A.M. when you turn the corner on a dark street and see the silhouette of a person coming toward you and you must decide in half a second whether to run like *hell*.

Apparently this skill springs from deep within your lizard brain, because when you apply conscious, deliberate thought to determine whether you actually have a rapport with someone, it screws things up. When Dr. Bernieri trains students *how* to make quick judgments, what to look for, to use their upper brains, and so on, they can't do it. (They can only make fast judgments by *ignoring* his instructions.)[3]

---

3. Dr. Timothy Wilson, professor of psychology at the University of Virginia, has found exactly the same reaction as Dr. Bernieri: that when people *try* to be introspective when making judgments, they are less happy with the results than if they "just went with their gut." In *The Wall Street Journal*, Dr. Wilson said, "We should let our adaptive unconscious do the job of forming reliable feelings and then trust those feelings."

"So, Doc," I say, "when a woman has cocktails with a guy and comes home and calls her friends and deconstructs the red-hot molten core of every single second of the evening, does all this thinking ruin the Snow White Effect?"

"No. It enhances whatever impression she got."

"And what happens if she lathers up all the possibilities *before* meeting a man on a blind date? Like should she wear her black taffeta cigarette pants that give her rump a two-basketballs-bouncing-in-satin sort of look and play the whole "I'm-such-a-daring-sauce-box" routine, or wear the blue dress that shows her waist and do the whole "I'm-*sooooo*-impressed-by-you routine, or the—"

Dr. Bernieri cuts in.

"The guy's *only* going to pay attention to how she looks."

Silence.

"That's basically it," says Dr. Bernieri.

(Screaming) ***"All the stuff we women go through and it comes down to being cute?"***

"On the first date. Yes," says Dr. Bernieri

"I'm going to brain you!"

I didn't brain him and Dr. Bernieri replied, "*Obviously* relationships aren't based entirely on looks. There must be similarity in interests and values and those must develop over time. But in the research done on synchrony, the *responsivity* of a female to a male is very, very VERY important. In other words, the woman who really laughs at the jokes and is attentive is definitely a turn-on."

So that's it, Doll. The Man Catching Theory makes things so much simpler, doesn't it? You see? We live on quite a sexual little rock, don't we? And whatever else is going on, on the other stars and planets and Wiffle balls in the universe, *here* on Planet Man Catch-

ing, everything, whether obvious or oblique, is about females bewitching males and creating the next generation.

So, relax. Just be yourself. You don't have to try to come up
with lamebrain tricks to enthrall a man. As a matter of fact, tricks
work *against* you. And the best part? You already know one element of the theory works—the Snow White. You've probably had
it happen in your own lovely life several times. Whenever I see
my neighbor Mayneal Wayland, a young lady of 85, I get all
thrilled and happy. It's been like this from the moment we met 10
years ago.

And as for the instantaneous detonation with men—well, the
truth is, it doesn't happen that often (Ma Nature is a fastidious old
trollop; she created synchronizing for one purpose, juicy new gene
combinations, and she's nothing if not selective about *whom* you
lose your brain for); but when clicking *does* happen—one more personal example will suffice:

I first laid eyes on my second husband, John Johnson—yes,
the former news anchorman—at Elaine's Restaurant in New York.
We were seated at different tables about 25 feet from each other. I
was with Prince Solomon, the jarringly handsome grandson of Emperor Haile Selassie, and a member Ethiopia's royal family. (Indeed the lad is the future emperor if they ever haul out the ermine
and scepter again.) Anyway, John and I pushed our chairs back at
the same instant and gave each other a look—but such a look that
John jumped up from his table and followed me and the prince (to
whom he bowed—in all seriousness) out of Elaine's to get my
number.

It was, I can say without exaggeration, a Snow White avalanche.
(And we had a helluva great time and still jump out of our skins with
joy when we see one another. But we could not live together in the

same house ... the same town ... county, state, country, hemisphere, world, galaxy, universe.)

The Man Catching Theory, of course, is not foolproof. Nature's taken only a couple billion years to develop it, so it still has some kinks. Perhaps you will defy the Theory and meet someone and not "click" (like Al Pacino and Ellen Barkin in *Sea of Love*), and the second or third time you meet (like Al Pacino and Ellen Barkin in *Sea of Love*) both your brains explode. (Actually, Woody Allen and a greyhound-waisted Dianne Weist in *Hannah and Her Sisters* is an even better example. They endure one disastrous date, run into each other *years* later in a SoHo record store, and *Zazzzz!*) Or you may experience a mere I'm-sorta/kinda-interested click, move on, become engaged to another man, break up, meet the first guy again, and Boom! Or you may be knocked out with an I'm-fascinated-in-spite-of myself click and it will develop into love over the next weeks and months.

All I know for sure is somewhere between your heart and your head is a little place where an apple core is waiting to be—well, egads, *this* is an unattractive analogy—where a little apple core is waiting to be burped up, and *BOoourrP* love happens; and this book is going to show you exactly what steps to take so you will swiftly and surely arrive at this marvelous moment.

The *Mr. Right, Right Now!* Promise

If You Get out of Your Own Way, Landing a Man in the Next 6 Weeks Will Be *Unavoidable*

Let's review:

When you meet a man, and you like one another, you "click." The Snow White Effect takes you by the throats and practically *drags* you to the next step. And there can be no confusion or ambiguity about the "next" step, because three billion years of evolution have given you so many beguiling moves that if you simply remain true to yourself—just be yourself!—chances are good the miracle (the madness, the lunacy of lust . . . and eventually love) will happen.

The trick is to prepare yourself and be ready for it.

So here's the promise, Doll: If you acquire the right attitude (Week One), look good (Week Two), learn to laugh at your fears (Week Three), place yourself where there are hordes of handsome men (Week Four), *and* get out of your own way . . . *Mr. Right, Right Now!* will bring you your dream man in six damn weeks.

Shall we commence?

Part Two

After
we met, I had to
be *restrained* by
friends so I wouldn't
plague him with
phone calls.

Madonna

talking about her
husband, Guy Ritchie, in an
interview with the author in the
Blue Bar at the Berkeley Hotel in
London, where the author not only
spilled her cosmopolitan on
Madonna, but also stuck her
with the check

DEAR E. JEAN: I'm a bright 33-year-old woman with a great career. But I'm such a dismal FAILURE at romance, after trying everything possible, I've surrendered all hope. My biological clock is no longer ticking, it's a sonic boom. Please help!

—Torn Between No Lovers

TORN, YOU SILLY TROLLYMOG! Come, come, darling, if you've tried everything possible, it's time to try the impossible. That's what this whole book is about. Read on . . .

Week One:
Lashing Your Brain into
Man Catching Condition

Without Charles Lyell's *Principles of Geology* and Thomas Malthus's *Essay on the Principle of Population*, young Chuck Darwin would not have hit on his theory of evolution.

Without Darwin's *Descent of Man* and Frank Bernieri's research on "clicking" and "synchronizing," yours truly *would* have hit on a man catching theory, yes, but it would have been without the capital letters and would have been built entirely on the secrets of sexual selection being revealed to me through the millions of hits on GreatBoyfriends.com.

As I mentioned in the introduction, I had inadvertently started GreatBoyfriends.com, an Internet dating site, when I suggested in my *Elle* column that women get together and recommend their ex-boyfriends to each other. My God! It nearly touched off a riot! The morning the story landed on the front page of the London *Times*—causing the hits to zoom into the millions—not wishing to insult Fate (which was obviously working overtime), I got out of bed early (*viz*, before noon) and, still staggering from the pineapple martinis

I'd bathed in the night before, waddled to my iMac, turned it on, looked—looked again—and in the silent crunching of Internet code, I suddenly realized I was gazing at a magical transformation.

There it was: The human heart quietly oozing out its mysteries in ones and zeros.

Yes, I—a total imbecile—even I could not fail to grasp it. What I had always thought of as a tedious "database" designed by my lovely sister, Cande Carroll, was translating in front of my eyes the infinite ways women enchant men. I knew how C. Darwin must have felt sailing into the Galápagos on the *Beagle.* It was all vividly before me—I could track the precise kind of woman each man was attracted to, the number of seconds he was "caught" by her picture, how many women he was comparing her with, if he was crossing tribal, economic, racial, and class lines, and on and on. It was flabbergasting!

It was the drama of Man Catching being played out in quadrillionths of seconds. So, as I say, I would have had a nice little theory right there. I would have combined the rich information from GreatBoyfriends.com with the ten years of "hard" research from the thousands of letters flooding into the *Ask E. Jean* column (where I hear from readers that I should be dragged through Times Square by my eyebrows—if my advice doesn't work—or that I am smarter than Socrates, if it *does*). Fine.

But all this stunning data from GreatBoyfriends was putting me in a kind of Darwinian daze. I was ripe. I was very ripe. I was damn near rotting on the bough. Then one afternoon I was looking up my favorite Schopenhauer quote in Darwin's *Descent of Man,* and I'm browsing, and I read Darwin's line: "Both sexes . . . would choose their partners not for mental charms, or property, or social position, but almost solely from external appearance"—and Kaboom! It was like a falling into a vat of Häagen-Dazs. I saw in a flash I could meld

Chuck Darwin with the second-by-second GreatBoyfriends.com data. A couple days later I remembered Dr. Frank Bernieri from a Malcolm Gladwell piece in *The New Yorker*.

Thus the Man Catching Theory was born. I.e. (here's a lip-gloss of the Theory): You are endowed by nature with certain inalienable attractions; when you meet a man you like, these attractions draw him to you, and if he likes you, and you like him, you "click"; and if you click, this means you are "synchronizing"; and if you are synchronizing, you will have something strong to build on; and so, Dolls . . .

It is precisely 9:41 P.M. If you start following the principles of the Man Catching Theory right now, six weeks from today at 9:41-ish, men will be crawling across the floor on their hands and knees, moaning and screaming your name.

Of course, the unspoken assumption here is that you *want* a man moaning and screeching. I will disabuse you of *that* little folly in a minute. For now, let's just look at the two basic styles women use to land men. I'm an admirer—but not a *huge* admirer—of both.

The Offensive Style

Your Offensive Woman is a saucy, extroverted number who behaves like a can opener in the Man Supermarket. She never waits for a chap to find her, she finds the chaps wherever she happens to be. Her confidence alone makes other women flee town.

When the Offensive Stylist meets a man she likes, she goes at him like Saint Joan galloping toward Orléans. (The Bastard of Orléans said about "the Maid" in battle: "She at once seized her standard in hand and placed herself on the parapet of the trench, and the moment she was there, the English trembled and were terrified.") If that isn't as perfect a description of an Offensive Stylist as you're ever likely to see, I'll cut my hair in a bowl like Milla Jovovich.

We're not just talking about sexual aggression here. We're talking about a certain kind of smarts. Kathleen Turner in *Body Heat* had poor William Hurt rolling on the linoleum in a slobbering stupor before she allowed him to lay one trembling finger on her. (And like K. Turner, your Miss Off will reveal a streak of vulnerability—even if she has to manufacture it . . . even if she ends up looking like an H-bomb with a drop of dew rolling down the side just before it explodes.)

It's this "soft" streak that gives a man the delusion he'll be able to dominate her. He also deduces from it that she possesses mind-blowing sexual depths.

The pitfall of the Offensive Style? It's fleeting. It's mercurial. Nobody can pull off total confidence 24/7. It becomes a show, a put-up job. Plus Miss Off's impudence can be so scrotum-tightening and frightening, the fellows often run like terrified goats.

Susan Sarandon in *Bull Durham* is a superb example of a top-level Offensive Woman, as are George Eliot, Missy Elliott, Princess Diana (during her divorce), Catherine the Great, Colette, Greta Garbo at all times, ditto Dietrich, Jane Austen's Emma Woodhouse, Courtney Love, and Anne Baxter as the combat-ready Eve Harrington in *All About Eve* (whilst Miss Offensive herself, Bette Davis, twatted away playing Defensive Margo Channing.) Which brings us to . . .

The Defensive Style

Glancing, down-lashing, and the giggle-goo-goo are the hallmarks of your traditional Defensive Stylist. Again, I think she has merit, but not *big* merit. For example, a Defensive Stylist is standing in line at Starbucks. A handsome stranger comes up behind her and, putting down his gym bag, takes in her jeans, peasant blouse, and Creamsicle cowgirl boots.

"Hello," he says.

(Glance-and-down-lash from the Defensive Stylist.)

"Uh . . . ," he says.

(Glance-and-down-lash from the DS.)

"Never saw the line this long," he says.

(Glance-and-down-lash. Glance-and-down-lash. Glance-and-down-lash. Glance-and-down-lash from the DS.)

"You?" he says.

"Mmm . . . ?" she says.

"Have you ever seen such a long line in here?" he says.

(Shrug-and-down lash from the DS.)

"Wheeew," he says.

(Giggle-goo-goo. Giggle-goo-goo from the DS.)

"I *need* my caffeine," he says.

(Glance-and-down-lash from the DS.)

"I just came from the gym," he says.

"I know."

"You know?" he says, surprised.

"Your biceps" she says, dropping her eyes, "look like cannon-balls."

The long-established Defensive Style is excellent for demure, less outgoing (or highly manipulative) women. Yes, it stinks of rotting corset strings. Yes, it's terribly retro and embarrassing, but, in fact, it can be as powerful as an audacious Offensive Stylist creating an uproar in a fly-fishing shop with just a smile and an eight-foot fly rod.

Indeed, Miss D is quite capable of whipping up one of the tastiest Battle-of-the-Sexes banquets: She makes mystery (the foundation of romantic love) and produces a near psychopathic need in the male beast to tear away "the enigmatic veils," as the dastardly Marquis de Sade calls them, to discover (at last!) the smoldering Kumquat underneath.

And just as Miss O reveals a dollop of vulnerability, Miss D (if she's good) reveals a streak of grit or stubbornness or elusiveness and presents a nice challenge to the poor fellows. On the downside, the Defensive Woman can be a doormat, a phony, and will have to fake orgasms for the rest of her life. Agnes Wickfield in *David Copperfield* is a fine exponent of this classic style. Other world-class Defensive Players are Princess Diana (before her marriage), Bridget Jones (a magnificent competitor who masquerades as an Offensive Stylist, but actually plays defensive), and the Four Horsewomen of Apocalyptic Charm: Jane Austen's Anne Elliot, Jackie Kennedy, Halle Berry, and Cinderella.

Both your standard Offensive and Defensive Styles are dandy, and when the two styles are used in combination, they go far beyond either one in isolation (e.g., you get a Meg Ryanesque/Nicole Kidmanish mash of prudence and abandon). However—and here's the part I've been working up to—a *third* style exists. It not only seems to be totally disorienting to the male sex, it is also ten times better than the Offensive and Defensive Styles put together, and it is called . . .

The Man Catching Style

For the first time in recorded history, thanks to the stunning technology of the Internet and its ability to track and dissect a human male's thinking process—a database of the world's supreme methods of man capturing is available for our examination. And it is *quite* clear one style above all beguiles the male beast.

It is the style that wrecks a man's power plays, blinds him, suctions out his ego, and drops the poor chap in his tracks. This is the Man Catching Style, and it is near nuclear when employed by an expert.

The most famous and brilliant avatars of this style are Cleopatra (the woman had a nose like a coatrack and still blew away half the leaders of the known world), Beatrice in *Much Ado About Nothing*, Scheherazade of course, Princess Diana (after her divorce), Madonna (under restraints), Jane Austen's Elizabeth Bennet, Marilyn Monroe (when she was not on the Locked Ward), Sharon Stone, Katharine Hepburn, Jennifer Garner, and Miss J. Roberts.

The Man Catching Style is what you'll learn in *Mr. Right, Right Now!* and it will totally kick the ass of any man alive. And for this style, Doll, it is essential you understand one thing:

How to *Think* Like a Man Catcher

NOTE: I understand your problems with the term *Man Catcher*.
It implies a rash wanton, a "snagger," or worse, a "trapper."
But I use the term in the noblest sense of a nimble, witty woman
who can filch a man's heart when he's not even looking;
and frankly, no other term in plain English works so well.

There are seven deep and essential truths at the core of the Man Catching Mind-Set:

1. *You live a life of purpose and that purpose is not about men.*

2. *You do not adopt anybody else's way of doing things, but find your own way—including following/not following any so-called seven "deep and essential truths."*

3. *You do not give a big flying fart blossom what men think.*

4. *Whether men love you or hate you, you truly don't care (okay, okay, you do care, but you don't desperately care).*

5. *You do not fritter away your life worrying about the male beast and what he is "doing."*

6. *You know it is completely useless to take men seriously.*

7. *This attitude causes men to froth at the mouth like rabid skunks.*[1]

The loose-fluid-cool thing the Man Catcher's got going on is hard to describe, except . . . you know those scraggily gorgeous Swedish girls you see backpacking across Europe with their dusty Tevas and ice-blue sunglasses . . . the girls who pull jugs of Chianti out of their rucksacks and, tossing back kilometers of blond hair, gaze up at the sun and smile? Well . . . *that's* the kind of nonchalant, casual brain wave a Man Catcher is on, Doll.

Not the pathetic man-centered Dingbat-Brain-Wave vibrating in the skulls of many American women . . . who are, by the way, every bit as beautiful as the aforementioned sloppy Swede girls, but who've become so frantic reading all the news reports about why they don't have boyfriends, men can pick up more laid-back vibes in the rip rooms of Brazilian waxing establishments.

The Man Catcher is engaged with life, but *detached* from "getting," etc., etc., "snaring," etc., etc., a man—consciously, deliberately *de*tached. As if she doesn't give a big rat's ass about the

---

1. Not that a decent guy *can't* be snared by a woman who takes men seriously. A pretty girl of 29 who takes men seriously will trap a $37,000-a-year assistant manager of the Olive Garden, no problem. (Which is good because chicks who take men seriously end up playing/paying for food anyway.)

"outcome" of her love affairs or where they are "going." (And, of course, the secret is, she really *doesn't* give a rodent's rump about the outcomes of her love affairs, which is why her love affairs are usually so satisfying and enduring.)

This kind of detachment, naturally, is an insanity-producing situation for your big league man.[2] But if you are NOT a nonchalant, cooler-than-a-polar-bear's-teat-type woman, if you were born with an extra volt of vivacity, if the blood in your veins runs at the temperature of molten lava, if your excitement-detector needle is always vibrating in the "Hoo-boy!" range, it is ridiculous *playing* it nonchalant. Be yourself. You can be detached *and* animated. It's all about the aura. And the aura radiates that you are not desperate.

Let Us Now Pause and Throw a Kiss to the Man *Loser*

The poor twit. Her thoughts are all about men. She sweats. She clings. She cries after sex. Show her a pair of old Calvin Klein briefs and tears spring to her eyes. Yes, she suffers unceasing agony on account of the male beast. "Because of men" every black minute she spends on earth is an unending torment. Even when she meets a

2. E.g., an "interesting looking" but by no means beautiful, 38-year-old Man Catcher who doesn't put on an act and enters the game detached will land herself a 37-year-old, $788,000-a-year advertising VP without a blink.

Why?

There are exceptions, but generally speaking, the higher up the salary scale the male beast is, the cleverer and more complex and cultivated he will be . . . and the cleverer and richer and more complex he is, the more sought after he'll be by women, and the more sought after he is by women, the more he'll be enticed by the disruptive force of the Detached Man Catcher.

nice gent and she manages to contain herself, and her opening moves are as cool as the goose bumps on Catherine the Great's backside, two weeks into a romance she is snuffling and blubbering and only thinking about what *he* wants, what *he* wants, what *he* wants. Her vision goes foggy. Her brain takes on huge rolls of Man Fat. Her playing field, instead of encompassing the whole world and all its *fantastic possibilities*, shrinks down to a strip of AstroTurf, on top of which somebody's left a big hamper of jockstraps.

There is always something ridiculous about a woman who takes men seriously. But a woman who is detached . . . un-manned . . . has something grand and beautiful about her. The minute—the instant— you're hooked on men and start caring about what the buggers think, there is not a man on the planet who won't varnish the court with you.

Which brings us to our Number One Law in the *Mr. Right, Right Now!* universe:

Man Catching Law #1
Men Want the Women They Can't Have.

Ergo . . .

Man Catching Law #2
(Stay with me on this, Doll)
If You Don't Want a Man,
Then That Means That Man Can't Have You,
And If That Man Can't Have You,
He Will Sweat
Beads of Testosterone
the Size of Ping-Pong Balls to Get You.

Men *live* for things they can't have.

All day long they're coveting things they can't have: remote controls large as coffee tables, Dodge Vipers, *Maxim* vixens, $3,800 titanium golf clubs . . .

Even in church the poor fellows *hang* on stories about the chap who loses his sheep and "doth leave the 99 in the wilderness," and doth develop a jones for that sheep, and doth scramble all over hell and back till he findeth his little Mutton Chop.

In fact, as a Soon To Be Big League Man Catcher, you know the only reason a man *has* a brain is to whip out his Palm Pilot and make lists of stuff he doesn't have. So to repeat the *Mr. Right, Right Now!* equation:

Quit Men = Get Men

But How Can You, a Smart, High-Achieving Female, Detach and Quit Men When All (all!) You Want Is Marriage and Children?

I submit a hideous joke is being played on you *personally* by the gods.

I submit to you that a woman who's desperate to get a husband is a woman who's undermining her chances of getting a husband.

Ahem, I'm not a huge fan of marriage. Every morning when I wake up and realize I'm not married, I drop to my knees and thank God! Weird. Because my parents are deliriously happy after *sixty years* together. But I've lost the itch to be *joined* (which is even weirder because I was crazy about my husbands).

Freedom has become the main theme of my life. I'm stricken with freedom. I'd rather snap myself in leg shackles and send myself to Sing Sing, than marry. (Hence, I've received a veritable shitload of proposals, and perhaps we'll explore this shockingly arrogant statement in a later chapter.)

As the GreatBoyfriends.com data and ten years of *Ask E. Jean* letters make clear, marriage just *can't* be the goal, Doll. A wedding will happen as a consequence of a rich and glamorous life. Let me repeat: When a nice fellow desires to settle down and start a family—desires it with every drop of his bachelor blood—that's exactly the fellow who'll run like a banshee when an overanxious husband-hunting junior partner from the Kotex & Kotex law firm levels her sights on him.

So, here's the deal: Human folly does not impede the working of the Man Catching Theory. Every woman is born with attraction skills . . . so the Theory *can* work pretty much no matter how idiotically a man and a woman are behaving. Whether the Theory works as *brilliantly* as possible is another story entirely. If your brain is soaked in cotton balls of desperation . . . if all you can think about is men men men men and pulling a bunch of dingbat "tricks," frankly the Theory wants to get up and leave the room. The Theory works a million times better if you un-man yourself, clear your brain, and glory in yourself.

It's detach or die, Doll.

Man Frenzy Detox

So let's wrap up Week One and give you your assignment.

For the next seven days you will not think man, breathe man, flirt man, sleep man, or eat Chef Boyardee. You will go everywhere, do everything, try everything, live your life, but you will not bat so much as a left eyelash in the direction of anything that possesses a testicle anywhere on its body. You will don only Donna (or Vivian, Carolina, Miuccia, Jill, Anna, Vera, Nicole, or Stella). The paintings you contemplate will be by Frankenthaler, O'Keeffe, and Cassatt. If a movie features more than 100 human beings equipped with penises, you will not see it. You will read female authors only. If a male singer comes on the radio, you will switch stations. You will not pursue, poke, fondle, or probe any masculine entity in its privates. You will not eat nuts. If you bake me a cake, it will be Betty Crocker.

At first you will go crazy. You will suffer several days of Man Frenzy Detox. But never mind. Watch Roz Russell in *His Girl Friday* (but for godsakes, look at Ralph Bellamy, not Cary Grant) and read Jane Austen's *Pride and Prejudice* (Misses Russell and Bennet are two of the noblest examples of Detached Man Catchers in history). The fog will begin to clear after a time, and you'll be absolutely astounded at how weird and kind of *festive* the world looks. Then, Doll, when you make it through the seven days and reach the eighth morning . . . you will not stop. You will *stay* detached. You will not cease being yourself. You will not shut off your color and nuance, but you will de*fricking*tach. I realize it's difficult. I know it's going to cost you considerable emotional energy; but I believe detaching is your strongest shot and the bitchingest move you'll ever make.

DEAR E. JEAN: I haven't had a date for months. It's not that I don't want one, it's just that I'm not a beautiful woman. I'm past 30 and definitely do NOT look like a model. How can someone like me attract a good man?

—Homely and Hating It in NYC

HOMELY: You giddy baggage! A girl with guts is never too old or too ugly to get all the attention, champagne, men, chocolate, and marriage proposals she wants. We merely have to flog you into shape. Read on . . .

Week Two:
Snow White and the 7-Day
Pulchritude Plan

Now don't tell me you've already forgotten *what* the Snow White Effect is, Doll! It's Instant Attraction. Clicking. Synchrony. If a fellow likes the way you look, he will like you; if he likes you, he will find you intelligent and intriguing; if he finds you intelligent and intriguing, he'll feel energized, exhilarated, and sexy; if he feels energized, exhilarated, and sexy (and you like him), you'll synchronize; if you synchronize, this is a fellow who's on his way to falling to the linoleum and rolling at your feet. So there is no getting around it:

He Must Like the Way You Look.

Which means this week you will wield two opposing ideas: First, *you don't give a tsetse fly's turd what men think.* Second, *you're going to turn yourself into a Walking Death Blow to attract men.*

These two concepts do not have to be locked in mortal combat inside your skull. As Niels Bohr, the Danish physicist, once said,

"A great truth is a truth whose opposite is also a great truth." (And Nielsy has a good time coming his way, compliments of old E. Jean, if he ever comes back to life.)

Now here's the good news:

Man Catching Law # 3
No Need to Put Yourself Through an Atom-Smashing
Beauty Regimen . . . Because to Be Detached
Is to Be Unattainable,
and to Be Unattainable Makes You "The Ideal."

Beethoven dedicated his Piano Concerto no. 24 to a woman who was so indifferent to him, so detached, she became his "Perfect One." I've never seen the chick, she could have had a chin like a glockenspiel for all I know, the point is old Ludwig could not possess her. She therefore was a very huge, very deep deal in his eyes.

So, as per Man Catching Law #3, no need to kill yourself "changing your look" as the lady magazines call it.[1] The glorious

---

1. The uninterrupted stream of laceratingly perfect lovelies flowing from our magazines, our movies, our TVs, and our computers keeps upping the damn ante. Worse, the lovelies keep getting more and more lovely, with the lovelies from last week being not quite as lovely as the lovelies *this* week; and men, the idiots, are beginning to expect *us* to look like these gorgeous dipshits. It's detestable! It's infuriating! It's stupefying and sickening and nearly impossible to pull off. We're forced to keep focusing more and more on perfecting our "appearance," with an hour scarcely passing that some nose-hair-curling iron is not being hawked on the Style network accompanied by an interview with Greta Van Botox (as the divine Christopher Buckley calls her).

Anyone who believes women are not run ragged merely keeping up (I work at *Elle*, after all, and know the photographs of breathtaking models are tweaked to look even more breathtaking) has been drinking too often from her Paul Mitchell Awapuhi bottle.

Man Catcher does a few subtle things here and there,[2] and, boom!
The daffy bastards hand over their hearts. For example, one tiny,
subtle thing you could do is lose forty pounds this week. I will tell
you *how* in a minute, but first . . .

Do These 8 Things and You'll Look Better Than You've Looked in a Long, Long, Long Time

1.

Sleep 10 hours a night. I know, I know, you work 14 hours a day. But,
listen, if you do *nothing* else on the 7-Day Pulchritude Plan, sleeping 10 hours a night will give you a younger, juicier appearance—

---

2. If you try too hard, you end up appearing desperate and silly.

    Worse, the more sweat, tears, blood, and cash you put into tricking yourself out,
the more you'll *need* men to find you pretty, and the moment you need a man to find
you anything is the moment that man will step over you like milk spilled on the Flow-
GRiP. Better to paint your buttocks green and move to the Kerguelen Archipelago.

    Still more hideous, if you spend a big bag of greenbacks on French designers,
Portuguese manicures, Italian makeup, English kneecap blush, Russian armpit
sweat-gland removal, etc., actually pull together a "stunning look," and drop a chap
in his tracks, then you're seized with the scalding insecurity that he doesn't like you
for the real woman you are. And of course, he *doesn't* like you for the real woman you
are because he doesn't have the first fricking notion of the reality of the woman you
are, i.e., without your mascara, eyeliner, blush, concealer, and $88 worth of hair vo-
lumizers, so you end up hauling your hunkies out of bed every morning at some un-
godly 6:30 A.M. to stagger to the bathroom and apply the mascara, eyeliner, blush,
concealer, and volumizers before he rubs the sleep from his eyes. As Rita Hayworth
said, "They go to bed with Gilda, but they wake up with me."

    If I could just convince all women to lay the hell off (like the chic women of
Portland, Oregon), we could relax, Jesus!

that wide-eyed look that *everything's right with the world*. Plus, I swear to God, it will crank your wit, your taste, your energy, your tranquillity, and your sex appeal. Rampant sleeping! If you can't do ten hours, do nine. (If you can only manage eight and a half, you're a wimp—or a saint, i.e., a single mother. In Rome, female gladiators slept twelve hours a night.) Do it!

P.S. University of Chicago researchers have found that skipping sleep can make you *old*. Sleep four hours or less a night and your body will cease regulating hormone levels, start storing flab (probably due to a drop in the human growth hormone), and when you sit down, your thighs will spread over the chair like waffle batter.

2.

Ten hours, three pillows. Elevate your head and you won't have bags under your eyes when you wake up. Four pillows is better (but, ahem, not so great for your spine). Lifting the bed frame with a couple of thick phone books works. But the Craftmatic bed is best. Yes! I'm talking the old fogy bed. The one with the grinning geezers you see advertised on cable TV. The one that goes up and down, honey, and *vibrates* (and you *now* know why the old gals are smiling . . .).

But little will you suspect what ecstasy awaits you in this fricking bed! Egads! After a week you won't have a bag, circle, roll, puff ball, or frog pouch near your baby browns. If you're an athlete, your back will feel better, but screw your back—*you'll look better*, and did I mention it vibrates? I purchased mine for $900. The twin size starts around $450. And when men see the thing . . .

"Oh . . . and this is my bedroom," you'll say.

"Nice."

"Yeah."

"What's that?"

"My Craftmatic bed."

"Your what?"

"Craftmatic."

"Like those old people on TV?"

"It vibrates."

"!"

"It goes up and down."

"!"

"See, this is the control," you'll say. "You press this button." (The bed will start bucking like a bronco in a rodeo.)

"Omigod," he'll whisper.

"This is the 'wave' button," you'll say.

"Let me see that thing."

"Isn't it unbelievable?"

"Give me that thing!" He'll grab for the control.

"No."

"Give me that!"

(Laughter.)

"No, sir."

(A skirmish.)

"What do I press?" he'll say.

(Laughter.)

"EEEEeeeeeeeK! Don't press *all* the buttons."

(Squeals.)

(Laughter.)

(Later.)

"I'm *never* getting out of this thing," he'll say.

Hell, the guy will marry you just for your bed.

3.

Pull up your bra straps. Stand straight. It blasts you with radiance and adds a whole inch in height when you do. I'm such a loser I wear the Body-Rite Posture Pleaser—a two-pound weight slung between my shoulder blades to remind me to pull back my shoulders. An hour or two a day, and it works like a dream.[3] ($40; www. bodyrite.com; 254-933-7483 or 800-490-7483. By the by, Body Rite, Craftmatic, etc., are not paying me to say these things, which really sucks.)

4.

Take a look at your so-called skin "care" regimens. Scrubbing, rubbing, pulling, popping, tugging, turning your face up to an exfoliatingly hot shower, and so on is cruel, vicious, subhuman, dries out your skin, roughs it up, mangles it, and causes wrinkles.

The best routine to keep yourself younger than a dew drop: splash 98-degree water on your face. If you're puffy or have dark circles under your eyes—well, now, you're not elevating your pump-

---

3. I started strapping on the ol' Body Rite after I "appeared" at a Bloomingdale's/ Kenneth Cole/*Elle* event to answer questions from the audience. The following week, nice Ali McQuade from *Elle* sent me pictures. "Why is Ali sending me pictures of *Liz Smith*?" I said, fanning through the snapshots. (Liz looks pretty darn great, but she is 80 years old, for godsakes.) Then I realized the shots were of E. Quasimodo Carroll. I was on the phone to Body Rite at once.

kin on four pillows are you?—splash chamomile tea on your face (it reduces inflammation because of its anthemic acid, tiglic acid, vitamin A, and a bunch of other fascinating chemicals listed in *Prescription for Nutritional Healing* by James F. Balch, MD, and Phyllis A. Balch, CNC). Brew and keep the tea in the Frigidaire. Let your face air-dry; splash a second time with water, apply your moisturizer, let it set, then do your makeup, and *voila!* You look younger than the Michelin Baby.[4]

5.

Don't worry. These aren't quadrates you're supposed to check off each time you drink a glass of water. No. *These* are Margarita Boxes. Check one each day you drink a margarita. A woman needs fun or she looks bad.

---

4. I use, ahem, Vaseline as a moisturizer. I know, I know, you're shaking your head in horror and dismay (and when you get *your* book deal, you can tell me what *you* use). I tell you, Vaseline is brilliant. It doesn't have the word "line" in it for nothing. It keeps the nasty things at bay. The Harvard Women's Health Watch calls Vaseline the best product against wrinkling on the market. (Eucerin is also pretty damn fabulous.) I slather my entire self in Vaseline every night.

6.

Something red.

Something green.

Something purple.

Something yellow.

Something blue.

Something orange.

Something chartreusey.

Something dark green.

Something black/brown/beige.

Eat them or be ugly.

Fruits and vegetables are loaded with natural chemicals that nourish your skin, hair, nails, eyes, teeth, keep your clitoris crisp, and help protect against age-related hideousity. And, according to Jane Brody in *The New York Times*, they can actually *reverse* chronic or deadly diseases.

7.

Balls. Trust me. Giant balls, Babe. Balls you sit on. Get rid of your chair at work. Sit on a big ball. (A) It will be terrific for your back and posture. (B) You burn more calories because you're getting a workout bouncing and rolling; heck, just keeping yourself stable—not falling over—works your *core*, that means your abs, obliques, etc. And (C)—hold onto your seat!—your cellulite will decrease.

Yours truly sits on a big (blue) ball to watch TV and another ball (also big and blue) to work at my desk. Yes, I have blue balls all over my house. I also have no cellulite. I rest my case. I have many, many other flaws, of course, huge, disastrous, deplorable flaws, but the extraordinary beauty of my thighs *gets me through*. (www. Equipmentshop.com or 800-525-7681; order the physioball in 65 cm, $22.50 (if you're under 5'5"), or 75 cm, $27.25 (if you're over 5'6", though I think everybody likes my 75 cm best, and kids go absolutely mad for it); and no, these people are not paying me either. And buy the foot-pedal thing to blow the balls up, or you'll burst your lungs. **BUT GET ON THE PHONE AND ORDER YOUR BALLS! GOD KNOWS WHAT YOUR THIGHS ARE UP TO AS WE SPEAK!**

8.

And finally, look through your closets, living room, kitchen, bathroom, and office and throw out all the boring people.

If you only do these eight things, or even just a couple of these eight things, or, hell, just one of these things, or, really, if you just *read* the list of the eight things, you'll be better looking. Not ridiculously better-looking, but pretty good-looking anyway.

And now, Dolls, we may begin the 7-Day Plan. No gimmicks, no bells, no whistles, no pets. Strike that. There *will* be pets.

The 7-Day Pulchritude Plan

Day One
A League of Your Own

Today you will whittle your waist to the size of a whippet's by patronizing your local batting cage and swinging at 50 baseballs. You will wear something sporty—scarlet cap, pin-striped shorts, your hot Irish/Spanish/Jewish/African (your ethnicity here) blood in your cheeks. If there are any guys around (and there will be, but you won't care) you will swing at 75 balls. If the guys are cute and also appear to be rich, you will swing at 100 balls . . . or until you're cracking home runs longer and harder than Derek Jeter, whichever comes first.

If you need a batting guru to help you with "technical issues," you will ask a 12-year-old boy. Or better, you will bring a 12-year-old boy along as your coach, or perhaps your 8-year-old niece; it's up to you.

Today's other activities: Eat nine colors and sleep ten hours (don't worry about falling asleep; you'll be half-dead after your workout).

Day Two
The Mr. Right, Right Now!
Fabulous Food Plan!

Today you can eat whatever you wish for breakfast. For example, I suggest blueberry pancakes topped with butter and maple syrup, a quart of mango juice, half a honeydew with peach yogurt, two rashers of English walnuts, a Mexican omelette, a wedge of key lime pie, and a strawberry daiquiri.

There are only three rules:

1. You must be in the present moment for each bite.
2. You must actually taste each bite.
3. You must make each bite *real*.

Ready? Sit down in front of your pancakes. Ok. Now. Pick up the Wedgwood pitcher of maple syrup . . . ok, ok, so it's a brown bottle shaped in the goddess image of Aunt Jemima, so much the better.

Now squeeze the syrup over the pancakes. Look at it as you pour. It's almost like melted topaz, isn't it? Like liquid bumblebees, like the sunlight on the fur of a flying fox . . . well, perhaps you're not thinking of flying foxes, no, you're thinking of a maple tree on a hill in the spring—yes, a maple tree with a syrup bucket hanging off her trunk collecting her sap just for *you* and a bluebird is sitting on her branches and singing. And the bluebird makes you look at the blueberries, and as you pour, you're thinking, "Ye, gods! Nobody's seen a freaking blueberry till this moment!"

You find yourself seeing—*real-izing*—those beautiful, beautiful blueberries. And the pancakes themselves, why, if you look deeply enough, you can see veritable wheat fields, and the sun beating down, and the wind blowing and the wheat tossing softly, or, knowing you, the wheat is tossing violently, the wheat is in quite an uproar.

You get the picture.

Take a bite. I hope you have provided yourself with an amusing little napkin, because tears may come to your eyes because of the intense—I'm talking in-*goddamn*-tense—pleasure, and the fact that, perhaps, all your life you've been missing out. At any rate, the bite will be a revelation. A real world-clearer. Now. Take a look at the honeydew.

And so on.

About 10 bites like this and you'll not be stuffed exactly, but something will be occurring that rarely occurs inside a career-building, overstressed American woman—a feeling that in this particular place and time is almost historically unprecedented. And that feeling is contentment. And perhaps surprise at the realization that you had never *dared* to taste your food before, and this is how food tastes.

That's it. That's the *Mr. Right, Right Now!* way of eating. And that's the way to lose weight. The only thing faster would be if I came to your house and stapled motion sensors to your jaws.

However, the *Mr. Right, Right Now!* method is *very* difficult to pull off. You're not permitted to read the paper while you're eating or watch TV or listen to the radio or make notes in your journal or talk on the phone. You must be completely and absolutely "in the present moment." This requires just enormous amounts of concentration, and, frankly, it messes with your daily schedule. (I mean, really, when was the last time you devoted a full twenty minutes to breakfast without scanning the headlines, checking out Katie

Couric's tangerine-colored sweater set, and tapping your "to do" list into your Palm?)

So I suggest you follow the *Mr. Right, Right Now!* way of eating for one, possibly, two meals a day. Three meals—please, nobody could pull it off, except Thich Nhat Hanh himself. (Check out the admirable monk's *Essential Writings* to learn more about "being in the moment.")

Other weight-loss tricks that work:

1. *Eat everything, just not a lot. Do not "diet." For God's sake. You know there's research showing that dieting causes a hormone called ghrelin to rise in your body. Ghrelin slows your metabolism and interferes with your ability to burn fat. It also increases your appetite. Have you noticed that the more you diet, the hungrier you get? According to the* New England Journal of Medicine, *ghrelin may be the reason.*

   So do not deny yourself. The instant you deny yourself a certain thing, say Peanut M&M's, then Peanut M&M's become the chief thing you think about. You may never have thought much about Peanut M&M's, but when you tell yourself that you can not have Peanut M&M's, then that is when you lose all control and thrash around the supermarket floor like a shark, leaving only empty Peanut M&M's wrappers and cellophane in your wake. (Read the illustrious Viktor Frankl's Man's Search for Meaning. *Frankl was a psychiatrist who was imprisoned in Auschwitz. He explains that to be denied food creates a "general preoccupation with food." I beg you to read this book. He has many ideas about achieving happiness and success that can change your life in a brilliant My-Life-Is-Changing-As-I-Read-This-Sentence kind of way.)*

2. *If you go berserk and down a can of Pringles, so what? There's nothing in the world better than a can of Pringles. The cool thing is to stop after one can and not beat up on yourself. Beating up on yourself warps your fragile psyche and makes you feel like a loser, and when you feel like a loser, you will, of course, eat another can of Pringles to make yourself feel better, which actually makes you feel worse, so I suggest you either call me and I will come to your house and pull out all your teeth, or you should remove all items such as cans of Pringles from the house.*

3. *Brew yourself a pot of Skin and Bones tea. I can't prove it, but I think my concoction boosts metabolism. Buy a pound of the ugliest, gnarliest-looking fresh ginger you can find. Slice it up (about six long slivers), pour very hot water (not quite boiling) over it, throw in a couple of green-tea-with-ginseng bags, maybe a cranberry tea bag, and let the stuff steep for fifteen minutes. Take to work. Drink and be divine. Eventually waste away to nothing.*[5]

4. *The easiest trick to lose three pounds is to sleep three hours later than you normally do for three days running. It flummoxes the old hypothalamus (the region in the brain that controls appetite, sleep, thirst, etc.). Conversely, if you rise early,*

---

5. Ha! I'm a genius! I just saw that Wrinkle Guy, Dr. Perricone, on PBS saying that if you drink green tea for just two weeks—and do nothing else to diet—you'll lose seven pounds. He didn't give a reason. I think seven pounds sounds like a lot, but he is a god and who am I to argue? My guess is drinking green tea heightens your awareness, lifts your mood, raises your spirits, and when your mood and spirits are flying, you discover there are more delicious things in life than food.

you're famished. *Unfortunately hungry people around the world know this fact all too well. So this is what I propose: If you try the Three Pound–Three Hour–Three Day Weight Loss Plan, donate $20 to Oxfam (Oxfam.org) for each pound you lose.*

Today's other beauty operation: Deflab your upper arms and flatten your stomach with a 90-minute rock-climbing workout. And just let me say, if you don't find a rock located at an indoor/outdoor, mostly male rock-climbing establishment, I'm going to think you are the dumbest little Doodle Brain to scramble up the pike.

When you reach the summit of said geological substance in your Marion Jones–style, skintight, Mount-of-Venus gripping, goldenrod-hued leggings and old baseball shirt, shake back your hair and smile.

If you've never climbed before—good! Excellent! At about 22 feet, you will suddenly feel the awful pull of gravity. You will look down. Balls of perspiration will dapple your upper lip like dewdrops on a peach. You will hate—no, you will abominate, you will LOATHE the book *Mr. Right, Right Now!* and all it's stupid !%#$!&!! suggestions. You will also loathe that hag E. Jean and pray the authorities put her in Sing Sing and make her wear one of those orange outfits with drawstring pants.

"Need help?"

A man's voice. You will notice, in fact, several men ascending to offer their services. You will laugh and refuse all assistance because you could care less about men; but the handsomest fellow, perceiving that your lusty ego is about to get you killed, will say, "Allow me," and, without further ado, take you in his arms and carry you all the way back to his $8.9-million ranch in Venezuela.

Day Three
The Visit from the
Three (Relatively) Wise Men

You will invite three gentlemen to your house. These gentlemen will be your good friends, and ideally, they will come in different ages, sizes, races, and with wildly diverging points of view. One fellow, perhaps a neighbor, will be over seventy. Another will be close to your own age. And the third will be exploding with such virile teen sap in all directions, your dog will mount his leg and enjoy herself six or seven times before you are compelled to lock her in the bathroom.

Seat the three men at your kitchen table and serve them your famous cheese pizza casserole or, perhaps, your F. Scott Fitzgerald Chili (so hot that after two bites guests run and jump into a fountain). Tell the chaps they are all smarter than Mr. S. W. Hawking and that you, a mere woman, seek their advice. Then pull out your pictures.

These pictures are, in fact, ripped from the pages of *Allure*, *Bazaar*, *Glamour*, *Jane*, *Elle*, *W*, *Cosmopolitan*, etc. Explain to your guests that every once in a while you like to do a little reinvention and that you've selected these shots because (A) there's something you like about each—the model's hair color, the film star's shoes, etc.; (B) that you're considering trying the some looks yourself, and (C) you would be much obliged if the handsome gentlemen would give you their masculine opinions.

"How do you think I'd look in this dress?" you'll say, holding up a page with Heidi Klum wearing a classic, pelican-gray caftan, very "in" right now.

"Hmmm . . ."

"Uhhhh."

"*&%!!"

"♦♦"

(That's sound of the old guy's eyebrows crashing on his cheeks in a frown.)

"Ummm . . ."

"Can I have more chili?"

"Come on, guys . . . don't you *love* this dress?"

"The color . . ."

"Yeah, the color . . ."

"You'd look terrible in this dress."

"You mean if you saw me wearing this, you wouldn't ask me on a date?"

"I'm married."

"I know you're married, Moose Balls. I was maid of honor at your wedding. Perhaps you don't remember me. I was the one wearing puffed sleeves the size of air bags. Now, look at this picture. Why wouldn't I look good in this dress?"

"Don't like the color."

"It's blah."

"It looks like bird poop."

"Don't you have something in a different color?"

You leaf through your folder of shots and pull out a picture of Heidi in a gauzy, salmon-colored wrap-dress.

"Hot!"

"Yeah?"

"Hot!"

"♦♦"

"Yeah? Really?"

"Hot!"

"Very sexy."

"Yeah?"

"Jesus."

"Yeah? Would I look okay in this?"

"Hot!"

And so on through your folder. By the end of the evening you'll possess a clear idea of the masculine vision.

(We once tried the "masculine vision" thing on the old *Ask E. Jean* TV show. We gave a 26-year-old guy an *Elle* magazine and told him to chose the hair/outfit/shoes/etc. he'd like to see on his girlfriend. It so happened his girlfriend was quite a babe to begin with, being a tall, well-built Danish girl with long, curly blond hair. She arrived wearing sandals, a short denim skirt, and T-shirt. Her look was effortless and sunny. Unfortunately, after her boyfriend chose the styles he liked, we turned the poor thing over to army of hairdressers, makeup artists, and the *Elle* fashion editor to do her "over." By the end of the show, the young woman's hair had been slicked back, her eyebrows had been plucked and darkened to resemble turkey vultures zooming in for the kill . . . the outfit was perfect but so neoconservative George W. Bush was probably wearing it under his flight suit when he landed on that aircraft carrier. I thought she looked a fright. The guy, however, was in ecstasies! I was stunned. It was all I could do to keep him from tearing off her clothes on live television. *This* is why I'm suggesting you only show your guests clothes and ideas that *you* like.)

Now, if your three gentlemen are up for it, and nobody's pressed for time, throw on your three killing-est outfits (don't *buy* anything, just choose favorite stuff from your closet) and haul your carcass up and down the living room for a fashion show. In ten minutes, you'll know what's bewitching and what isn't.

P.S. Make your final outfit a pair of jeans, because you will need them for your next activity . . .

Tonight's workout: The motocross track . . . where, amidst the lush gas fumes, you'll see such an unbelievably dense concentration of the opposite sex, such an unruly mass of testosterone, such a rainbow of leather, I'm afraid you may never return home again.

If it's not a race night—and if you've never straddled one of these machines—you might be able to rent a bike (gloves, boots, jacket) and take a lesson. The next day you'll swagger into the office still wearing the helmet, smelling of motor oil, and bespattered with blood and Band-Aids. (When you do finally remove the helmet at lunchtime you'll be surprised to see your hair has grown five inches—from all the standing on end it was doing at the track.)

Guys at work will be impressed.

Day Four
Hair Day

I personally don't know a single thing about hair. My own personal hair always looks a mess. I can honestly say, Doll, please don't listen to me on this topic. Here's what you do: when you see someone's hair you like, ask them who cut/colored it and make an appointment.

Today's beauty tip: Cheap hair conditioner makes a lovely shaving cream for your legs.

. . .

Today's other beauty tip: Massage your scalp with your fingertips (not nails) when you get out of bed in the morning. It gives
body to your style (if unlike me you are lucky enough to *have* a
style).

Today's workout: Nine holes of golf. (Males outnumber females
on the links five to one, not that you care.) Or if it's cold, hit a $10
bucket of balls at an indoor driving range.

Day Five
Makeup Day

I don't know a thing about this subject, either. My blush is always
somehow turning into the color of a pot roast, and I usually have so
much mascara flopping about, I look like I've hooked mink tails to
my eyebrows. Do not listen to me about *makiage*, I beg you.

　　If you can afford it, book a makeup artist for a "play date."
(Don't know one? Call the top salon in town and ask for a referral.)
Or, you can schedule an appointment at your favorite department
store makeup counter and go for a free makeover. (Avoid lunchtimes
and Saturday afternoons, for obvious reasons.) Or simply leave work
at 9:30 A.M., treat yourself to a margarita, arrive at the store, scan all
the counters, and mosey up to the salesperson/stylist whose look
you admire. Bring pictures. Be nice. Tell the stylist you wish to try
something new/old/classic/less Bird of Paradise/more Catherine
Zeta-Jones/etc. If you're "on a budget," say so. Ask for samples. You
don't have to buy anything.

. . .

Today's beauty tip: Pink umbrellas! On a gray, wretched day, a woman smiling under a pink umbrella looks younger than the Little Mermaid.

Today's other beauty tip: Slather your mouth with hydrous lanolin every night ($2.99 at any drugstore). Wake up with lips plumper than tennis balls.

Today's workout: Have you ever fired a weapon? Ever shot at anything? Wish to gain insight into the so-called "male mind"? (A boy begins playing with weapons early in his life, and this predilection lives on in the adult man's love of cars, motorcycles, sports,— really, I don't need to point out something so observable, do I?)

So today's the day. Visit your local gun club, skeet club, or firing range. (Call your local hunting-and-fishing store for a referral.) Not only will marksmanship fundamentals (i.e., taking a steady position, aiming, breathing, squeezing the trigger) teach you how to hit a target—invaluable basic training for bringing down the male beast—there's also a strong probability you'll be the only woman there.

Day Six
Ensnaring the Dizzy Buggers

This is a big day, an exhaustive day, in many ways a hideous day. Today you must be ready and willing to try on every item in your closet. If this means you have to empty all your T-shirt drawers, turn the contents of your jewelry box out on the bed, pull down your sweater shelf, go without food, without water . . . if you must don 160 different outfits and find a dazzling combination and have to walk around outside and be followed by rich men and chased by rock stars, and if this means the street in front of your house will be littered with the bodies of men who've shot themselves because they can't have you, then *you must be prepared to make the sacrifice.*

These are the components of a great Man Catching outfit:

1. *The male beast is hardwired to chase the feminine shape. Whether you are 208 pounds or 108 pounds, curves captivate the giddy doodlebangers. Especially the all-important waist-hip ratio. So bait the trap. (I'm using the plain Anglo-Saxon here.)* Show your waist. *You don't have to do a whole Shakira number—a dress that just skims your figure like the demure dress worn by Diane Lane in* Unfaithful *in the café bathroom scene is perfect.*

2. *Men are attracted by color. It's love at first* sight, *not love at first sound. So catch their eye with reds, pinks, purples, any hue that enhances your eyes. As Chuckie D. says in* The Descent of Man, *a chap's senses "are so constituted that brilliant colors . . . give pleasure."*

3. *If you have decent legs, wear a sarong skirt so short your fanny thinks you forgot to get dressed. If your thighs are not your comeliest asset, then something below the knee. Experiment. Any skirt that wraps, swings, flutters, floats, or flips around like a veil will toss a guy's confetti.*

4. *Show the arch of your foot. A really great pair of Jimmy Choo's or those witty (and incredibly cheap) espadrilles from Wal-Mart can make you look more naked than if you have on nothing at all. Remember, it was the* slipper *that brought the marriage proposal in* Cinderella. *Not the dress.*

5. *Pull up your (aforementioned) bra straps. If your breasts aren't high enough to comb your hair with your nipples, then by all means hoist them again.*

6. *Smell bewitching. I recommend combining fragrances from Jo Malone. (I realize all the magazines advise creating a "signature" scent. I find that a bit Grandma. To be sexy, surprising, criminally attractive, wear the same base scent like Honeysuckle & Jasmine, then slither on a top note, like Nutmeg one evening, and Amber and Lavender the next.)*

7. *Your curves/age/race are appraised by men in seconds. Then the details of your hair/face/class/education/bloodlines are taken in—less quickly than you are assessing their face/bloodlines, etc.—but supremely quick nonetheless. So dress how you wish to be perceived.*

8. *This last point is so important, it's a Man Catching Law:*

Man Catching Law #4
Delight in Your Own Attractions,
and You Will Attract.

It's as simple (and impossible) as that. There's no such thing as an "ugly" woman. (There are *geniuses* at being scared of their own beauty.)

I once saw a plain girl at a bar in Chelsea. Everything about her was dull as a nun's underwear drawer, except her $300, white Ralph Lauren shirt and her vaguely erotic tight, black skirt. She was obviously just coming from the office (or convent), and instead of sitting at a table, she took a position at the bar with a friend, turned, and scanned the room with a bored expression. Her eye landed on the man I was with.

He was famous, needless to say.

She straightened and smiled at him. He smiled back politely, and in the next instant (my iMac keyboard is getting warm even as I type this) she was transfigured into a . . . well, not a radiant beauty, hell, not even a beauty, but something better than a beauty—a *siren.*

With a small, swiveling movement of her torso, she twisted slightly away and tilted her face downward so it was concealed behind her dead-leaf-brown, shoulder-length hair. Then with a lifted hand, with a gesture of drawing back a curtain, with the slowness fit to inflame a dead man, she raised her head, rolled her hair back from her face, opened her eyes wide as sandwich plates, and gazed at my boyfriend. It was one of the sexiest moves I have ever seen in my life.

This was a woman who *wallowed* in her attractions.

Then, by God, if she didn't drop her head again, disappear behind her veil of what *now* appeared to be a veritable *mane* of chestnut hair gleaming with indescribable luster, lift her hand, roll her hair to the *other* side, and, as I'm saying to myself, "O dear, O goodness, somebody *turn her off*," if the little Man Chomper didn't gaze back at him out the sides of her lashes! I was torn between admiring her and wanting to strangle her.

Her spirit inspired me with great respect. Yes. But I lost no time in removing the famous boyfriend from the premises, lest he fall to his knees and propose to her on the spot.

So. Let's wrap this chapter up by stripping off our clothes.

Yes, go ahead. I'll wait. Ok? Now, go stand in front of the mirror. Don't worry—I'm not going to give you any chickenhearted crap about "loving" and "accepting" your body. No. No. No. What I want you to do is take a long look.

Are you looking? Fine. Now admit it. Isn't your body the funniest goddamm thing you ever saw in your life? (My own body looks like I ate my comforter for dinner.) So don't hold back—*laugh*. If you are so inclined, roll on the floor. I'm serious. One good laugh is worth three years of hand-wringing about whether *men* find your legs attractive.

Laugh at your naked self every night for the next five weeks, and soon you'll be filled with joy, not anxiety, at yourself. Why? Anytime you can laugh, Doll, you've got the world by the ass.

DEAR E. JEAN: I had a Sleeping Beauty fantasy, but now I'm beginning to understand my prince is NOT coming to wake me. I'm very attractive and quite intelligent, but I have trouble even STARTING a conversation with a man, much less getting a date. How do I get over my fear? —Paralyzed in VA

DEAR PARALYZED: You don't want to get over your fear, Honey Poo, you want to USE it—distill it, bottle it, put a cap on it, set it on your dresser, and let the sight of it fill you with power. Read on . . .

Week Three:
What to Do When the
Freaking-Out Thing Kicks In

So what if you tremble like a tomato aspic on a plate when you meet a fellow? The Man Catching Theory works whether you're frightened or not (if you're being yourself, a little frazzle makes you slightly *more* stimulating, not less). It's the BIG fears the Man Catcher must rid herself of—the fears that come with the lifetime warranties. So, ahem. Come out from under the bed, Fear, you bastard, this chapter is about you.

After some hesitation, asking me for "a moment" (I can hear the surprise in his voice), Fear creeps out—*glides* out, really—and frowns at me. He is short and plump, sort of Danny DeVito plump, and pale, very pale—very un–Danny DeVitoish complexion-wise. Fear is, in fact, as pale as a maggot. Perspiration spatters his high forehead. His eyes—one icy blue, one turdy brown—go off in two different directions.

Fear adjusts his tie. The fellow is suavely attired, I must say! White Armani suit, raspberry-and-cream-stripped shirt, violet tie with a scorpion stickpin, heliotrope vest with magenta piping, burgundy shoes with lilac spats, and sporting—is that the word? flour-ishing? wielding?—an ebony walking stick with a silver handle carved in the image of Angelina Jolie.

I ask Fear to sit down.

He lowers his big fundament on the edge of the Craftmatic bed, removes his homburg, and wiping back his hair, which is sticking to his forehead, he says:

Fear: What do you want? AFRAID you won't get this feebleminded book done on time?

Eeee: Afraid? Don't underestimate yourself, Mr. Nerve Rack. I'm damn near paralyzed.

Fear: Calm down, I've read your first two chapters.

Eeee: Well . . . ?

Fear: Well . . . since you <u>ask</u>. I've been puking up my guts ever since.

Eeee: Must be *careful* of your lovely spats.

Fear: I've upset you.

Eeee: I'm not upset.

Fear: You look upset.

Eeee: I'm not upset.

Fear: You look it.

Eeee: I'M NOT UPSET!! And incidentally, fuck you.

Fear (smiling)

Eeee: Right. Here we are in Chapter Three, which is all about you, Mr. Fearsome. So, I'd like to ask you a few questions. What would you say about that?

Fear (shrugging, but flattered): Proceed.

Eeee: I've got my tape recorder going. Mind?

Fear (shrug)

Eeee: Excellent! Good! This could be fun, huh? A little *frisson*. So! Ahem! Please tell me about yourself.

Fear: I've been interviewed by writers a thousand times more talented than you.

Eeee: I have no doubt. No doubt at all. I'm extremely obliged to you for condescending to speak with me. If you would kindly indulge me, Fearsome, this is a list of the "Typical Fears" that besiege an intelligent woman when she's "looking for a mate."

Fear: My prime area!

Eeee: Don't I know, you naughty rogue!

Fear: You're doomed.

Eeee: *Who's* doomed?

Fear: You, Madam. Smart women, fast-track women, elite women. Every single one of you pathetic twit-wits. Doomed!

Eeee: Now, now, now, Mr. Perspiration. Nobody's doomed.

Fear: Horse manure, Madam.

Eeee: For the first time in history gigantic numbers of women are successful, rich, autonomous, and sexually liberated.

Fear: Bovine excrement, Madam!

Eeee: Our clothes are stunning. Our apartments are spectacular. Our travels make Marco Polo look like an agoraphobic. We go where we chose, we do what we like, we snog whom we please.

Fear: Is this Tampax commercial over?

Eeee: We are F-R-E-E.

Fear: And what, may I inquire, are you doing with this freedom?

Eeee: Changing the world.

Fear: Ha! (laughing and coughing fit) Stop! You're killing me! You're the funniest dame I've ever—I hope you're being sarcastic, Madam.

Eeee: I'm dead serious.

Fear (snorting): What you broads are *really* doing is running around looking for Mr. Right so you can ditch all the freedom, settle down, and breed.

Eeee: Oh please. American women have enough power to love men, bear children, and thrive in brilliant careers. Hush up. Now. (sounds of papers flapping) Shall we begin with the list of "Typical Fears Encountered by the Smart Woman Whilst Looking for Mr. Right?" Number one—well, mmm. I see these fears are not in order. Should we just start with the top one?

Fear (crossing his legs smugly): Whatever.

Eeee: A woman who's thirty years old has been dating for fifteen, sixteen years. At least. That's fifteen or sixteen years of accumulating romantic terrors—

Fear: The main terror being she's *thirty*.

Eeee: But at least she now *knows* what works and what doesn't, right?

Fear: How can she know what works when I'm reducing her to such self-hating stupors after each love affair? She makes the same mistakes every time! It's magnificent!

Eeee: But what happens if she doesn't do that?

Fear: But she always does.

Eeee: But what if she simply stops being freaked-out and *uses* all these frightful experiences? Don't losers learn better than winners in war? Aren't mistakes better teachers than victories?

Fear: In war, yes. In the battle of the sexes? It's my duty to pulverize a woman's self-confidence till she loses all trace of her spine and turns into just another tedious neurotic.

Eeee: But can't smart women learn from *that* too?

Fear (rolling his eyes in two different directions)

Eeee: The more action we take, the less afraid of YOU we'll be?

Fear: This is old stuff, Madam, really—come on.

Eeee: And taking action against you is a skill? And that it can be learned? And that it can be increased by experience? And that—

Fear (shrieking): What . . . in . . . HELL is *that*?

Eeee: You've never seen a Great Pyrenees dog?

Fear (backing up on the bed): It looks like a Lipizzaner.

Eeee: Why, look at that. She likes you! My goodness, she really loves—good lord! Down! Down, girl! Down, Alabaster! Well, I've

never seen her, uh, *enjoy* herself so, uh, romantically, before. Well—!
Oops! Bad Alabaster! Bad! Bad! You naughty girl! Give Mr. Fear
back his toupee!

Fear (gasping): Get her off!

Eeee (laughing)

Fear: I beseech you, Madam!

Eeee: (escorting Alabaster out; shutting the bedroom door): In my
opinion you look handsomer without it. Here. Look in the mirror.

Fear (examining his bald head, unsure): Really?

Eeee: Very Vin Diesel. What a stroke of luck! Turning adversity to
victory! This calls for a bottle of champagne!

Fear: For God's sake! Don't leave me here alone! Shouldn't you lock
the door?

Eeee: Don't worry. Alabaster won't be back. She's run to the garden
to bury your hair. So my question is, how do we lash ourselves into
action when we're facing you?

Fear: You're asking ME, Madam?

Eeee: Yes. Fearsome, my man. Just give me two or three suggestions,
two or three darts from your huge arsenal of weapons. It will make
the battle so much more interesting!

Fear: I . . . I . . . I . . . I'm afraid to tell you.

Eeee: Fear dear, please. Do be serious.

Fear (tempted but hesitating): You'll never believe me if I DO tell
you.

Eeee: Try me.

Fear: Okay. I'm powerless against a woman who's just eaten two packages of Oreos and a can of Hershey's syrup.

Eeee: Nice try, Mr. Reeking Crotch!

Fear: I'm a total pushover.

Eeee: Here's what I'm thinking. Being in powerful physical condition gives a girl grit. Tennis, volleyball, downhill racing . . .

Fear . . . napping . . .

Eeee . . . soccer, karate, fencing . . .

Fear . . . sweater de-pilling . . .

Eeee . . . basketball, judo, softball, boxing . . .

Fear . . . pot-smoking . . .

Eeee . . . badminton—*do you mind,* any sport where we can project our fears onto our opponents is good, because it trains us to fight you, Mr. Weep & Pule. Competition pushes us. Lifts us above ourselves.

Fear (utter silence)

Eeee: Well . . . ?

Fear: Naw. Instead of batting a shuttlecock, you should bat your eyelashes. Smart women, Madam, are *scary* women. You intimidate men.

Eeee: But sports—

Fear: *Forget* sports. Major blocks of time must be employed in making yourselves beautiful. *That's* what men want. Worry about your weight more and your jump shot less. That is, if you have any sense whatsoever, which is—

Eeee: You're so adorable when you lie, Mr. Sweat Gland! Little beads of blood form on your forehead. I'll tell you what else I'm thinking. I'm thinking that taking action against you means possessing an awake brain. So we should get lots of sleep and not live on globs of slop—dumb TV, dumb magazines, dumb grub.

Fear: Oh, please . . .

Eeee: And I think if we—

Fear: We're getting a turdload of *your* thinking, aren't we, Madam?

Eeee: Anyway, if we maintain a comic attitude toward you, toss off a well-aimed laugh in your face, and so on, I believe you'll run like a diseased rat.

Fear: Look, you got any more stupid questions? This is beginning to look suspiciously like a FORMAT to me.

Eeee: If you answer the next question without lying, Mr. Falsie Man, I'll let you run the Craftmatic up and down a full minute.

Fear: Three minutes.

Eeee: Two minutes, baby. Ready? Okay. In today's society—

Fear: "In today's society"? No, Madam. Any question beginning with "In today's society" is more tedium than I can possibly endure.

Eeee: Oh? And what if I just take away your walking stick and poke you in the testicles?

Fear: Now, now. Get on with it. And don't ask me any of your imbecile questions about chasing men.

Eeee: We never chase. We place ourselves in their *vicinity*.

Fear: You want a tip? Men are just as afraid as women. Maybe more. But they present themselves as being less afraid. But it's all a show. Remember. *All a show.*

Eeee. Oddly enough that hideously repugnant news gives me hope.

Fear: Don't mention it.

Eeee: So. Once she's in the vicinity, how can a smart, but shy, woman overcome you, Fear, and strike up a conversation with a man she likes?

Fear: Naw, naw. Little Mole Women must stay in the house and not go lurching around outdoors latching onto fellows' pant legs and spilling their guts nervously about the weather.

Eeee: Give me that Craftmatic control, Mr. Neck Welt! Whoa! What's this?

Fear: Nothing. Let go of my hand.

Eeee: No, no, no, let me see. Hold still. Why, you've chewed your nails down to little slits! Little nubs! Judas! The ends of your fingers look like throw pillows. Egads! Look at your thumb, poor thing, I can't even *see* the nail. What? *Come on.* It vexes you that I'm holding your hand? It embarrasses you? You're feeling a surge of traumatic emotions? Your hand is shaking. But, Fear dear, don't you know how charming you are when you let your vulnerability show?

Fear: Nawwww . . .

Eeee: Ye gods, Fearsome, you're practically . . . irresistible. Look at you.

Fear: Nawwww.

Eeee: A shy woman should do just what you're doing now. She shouldn't be afraid to show she's afraid. You know why? Shy people possess a striking advantage. They make excellent listeners. Nothing makes a chap fall in love like hearing himself talk.

Fear (taking back his hand): Would to bloody God that you, Madam, subscribed to that theory.

Eeee: Ok. Ok. Ok. Ok. Ok. Ok. Ok. All a shy woman has to do is (A) stop imagining the worst; (B) cease thinking about herself; (C) think of *other* people.

Fear: No, Madam. She's a Mole Woman. She'll never give up her paralyzing self-obsession.

Eeee: But . . .

Fear: No buts. She'd be better off in her "spectacular" apartment, taking a big risk and spending Self Time every morning owning her feelings, getting in touch with her authentic person, and journaling in a nonjudgmental, sympathetic, and centering manner.

Eeee: One more moron remark like that, Mr. Dick Quiver, and I'm calling the dog. Wait—why are you looking at your watch?

Fear: Time to knock it off. I have work to do. People to see.

Eeee: Oh, no! Stay! We're just beginning to become acquainted. Stay, Fearsome. Our *frisson* and all that. Wait! Don't go. I want to run my Week Three assignment by you.

Fear (sitting reluctantly): Well, go on.

Eeee: It seems to me that this third week, the Lovely Reader should strap on a parachute, climb to 12,555 feet, and jump.

Fear (ruminating): The Lovely Reader will never do it.

Eeee: But it's the single best way to deal with you, Fearsome. Right? Because once the Lovely Reader hurtles toward planet Earth at 125 miles an hour, not a damn thing can ever scare the Lovely Reader afterward. Candace Bushnell, the dashing author of *Sex and the City*, and I once did it out in California.

Fear: I was there. I recall that Candace was smashingly costumed in a red jumpsuit. You, of course, vomited all over that blue thing you were wearing.

Eeee: The point is, I did it. And that should be this week's assignment.

Fear: Come, come, Madam. You only did it because you and Candace hired your own personal video photographers to photograph every single second of it.

Eeee: Well, the thing is, these parachute places have professional jumpers who hook themselves to your back so you absolutely can't get killed. Anyway, I think it's a superb Week Three assignment.

Fear: Not bad.

Eeee: Because after I did it, I noticed that you, Mr. Fearsome, don't come around as much anymore. I mean you're around all the damn time, of course, to keep me sharp, but now it seems you're a little more laid-back.

Fear (standing, adjusting his tie): Thank you, Madam. You know it's rare I receive a kind word. And in return, I will tell you something true.

Eeee (rising and gazing down at the top of Fear's bald head): What is it?

Fear: Bend closer.

Eeee (bending)

Fear (clearing his throat): Closer.

Eeee (bending closer)

Fear (whispering): You need to lose eight pounds.

Eeee: You filthy cad, come on! You were going to tell me something deep! Something important. I could see it in your eye. What was it? Tell me. Tell me, you fiend. Or do I have to whistle for a certain hirsute toupee rustler?

Fear: Ok. Ok. It's just this. People are only frightened because they *perceive* things as frightening. I am *perceived*. I am not a fact. Look at me. Do I look fearsome?

Eeee: At some angles you look like Supreme Court justice Ruth Bader Ginsburg.

Fear (rising): Thank you.

Eeee: Huh? Wait a minute, don't go. Wait. You mean if we change the way we look at things—things change? Let me get this straight. If—

Fear: There's nothing to get straight. Your fears of the world around you are arbitrary. All that bull crap imprisoning you? Arbifreaking-tary. Well, nice talking to you.

Eeee: Wait. Wait! Wait! Wait! One more thing. The subtitle of this book is "How a Smart Woman Can Land Her Dream Man in **6** Weeks." Every now and then I burst into big red welts when I think of it. Is it possible? Can a woman actually land a man in six weeks?

Fear: When a man falls for a woman, it happens in less than a minute. The main fear, Madam, is *not* finding the fellow.

Eeee: Aha! That's all in the next chapter! The 119 best places to meet men. Hang around, Fearsome. We'll go over it together. Wait! Wait! No! Don't go!

Fear: Be seeing you, Madam.

And with that, Fear crossed to the window, drew up the sash, and after looking around for the dog, squeezed over the sill and disappeared into the woods behind my house.

DEAR E. JEAN: I've spent more than $2,000 on a dating service that's so far brought me four Mr. Wrongs. I try to meet guys. I've tried the club scene, car washes, coffee shops, book clubs, you name it. I'm confident enough to know I'm attractive. But it's just so hard when there's something I want so badly (marriage and children) but can't find it. How much longer do I have to tell myself "It will happen"? —Lonely Girl

MY DEAREST GIRL: By the Burly Nipples of Emily Brontë! Not even the author of W. Heights would look for a man in a book club. Most book club members are females. It's a waste, waste, waste of your time! Here's the deal . . .

Week Four:
The 119 Best Places to
Meet the Male Beast

The Internet

In the first draft of this book, which I lashed together many months ago . . . Ok, Ok, let's not start off with an exaggeration.

I didn't "lash" it together exactly. It was more like I *lugged* it; the point is, I was trenchant! I was on it! I'd amassed 118 groovier and groovier places to meet the chaps and then climaxed the whole thing like a fool with one hairless little footnote on "Internet dating."

And I was reluctant to include even *that*. I was wary of on-line personals. The stacks of horror-infested nightmares on my desk— i.e., letters from women who'd met men through the Internet, fallen in love, and the louse bags turned out to be married, or *worse* (like that snork-horned army colonel who proposed to fifty . . . well, ad- mittedly they must have been *exceptionally* naive . . . women)— gave me the creeps. I couldn't help picturing a short, bald, monstrously fat wanker in his malodorous boxers hiding behind his

computer screen, preying on the sweet virgin flesh of etc., etc., . . .
when HIZZZ-ZOOK!

I started an Internet dating site.

I had no idea what I was doing. I just wanted to help a few *Elle*
readers who'd been plaguing me (E. JEAN! YOU FEEBLE-
MINDED MORON! GET OFF YOUR FLABBY BUTT!) and find
them boyfriends. So I simply asked women to recommend the handsomest, nicest, richest single fellows they knew to other women—
and kaboom, GreatBoyfriends.com was born. My sister, Cande
Carroll, an elegant geek, normally a prudent little creature, engaged
to be married to a doctor of economics, went insane, got the thing up
and running, and became the cofounder.

Now, you never saw two bigger imbeciles than Cande and myself, yet people fell hard for the site. They *loved* the idea of women
recycling (*"regifting"*) their men—"Take My Ex, Please" was the title of Ginia Bellafante's engaging *New York Times* article about it.
Cande and I had not yet ceased screaming and running mad over
the *Times* and a *Newsweek* article by Seth Mnookin, when *The London Times* put it on its *front* page, and this of course completely de-
prived us of our senses. (*That* morning I stared at the computer
screen and my brain snapped its panty girdle. I realized I could
track—through the second-by-second translation of ones and zeros—precisely how women "caught" men . . . oop, excuse me, I've
bored you beyond endurance with this already.)

The site was instantly perceived as "trustworthy." It was women
doing good deeds for womankind. It was women *vouching* for guys
they knew for a damn fact were true-blue valiant, outstanding fellows. (*Viz* . . . not Mr. Numb Nuts claiming to be a 6'2" triathlete
doctor—when in fact he was a 5'3" loser with bright red pimples all
over his back.)

After *The Early Show* AND *The Today Show* did big stories, followed by *The Los Angeles Times, 48 Hours,* and a system-crashing *Oprah* (so many people logged on at the same time, we came *this* close to knocking the entire city of Ithaca off-line), Cande and I have alternated between fainting on the sofa and staying awake around the clock trying to keep up with the astonishing million and a half hits a day.

We also did not let the gigabytes grow under our feet. GreatGirl-friends.com was up and running soon afterward.

So, ahem, I, a onetime sourpuss, have become the country's— aw, hell, the *planet's*—leading expert on on-line dating, and I swear to Zero One (the goddess of the Internet), this is the cleverest way to meet the male beast. A few years ago you may have had a choice of twenty good guys. Now you have 200, or 2,000, or 20,000 delectable fellows; and I'm convinced it's as safe as meeting the huggers at a church social. Why? Because by the time you agree to a rendezvous, you should have exchanged enthrallingly large amounts of information and know if you share the same interests and values.

Plus there's something girlish and adventuresome about slipping out the window of your tight demographic, jumping the barricade of your social circle, and e-mailing a handsome stranger at 2:20 A.M. And the Internet is probably the very *best* way for a shy (or reserved) woman to cut through the superficiality and shallowness of day-to-day existence and allow the depth and glory of her personality to blaze forth. The young evolutionary biologist Olivia Judson has an intriguing perspective:[1]

---

1. Judson is a leggy Brit with a doctorate from Oxford, author of the immensely entertaining and informative *Dr. Tatiana's Sex Advice to All Creation*—read it, it's hysterical; she's transformed up-to-the-minute Darwinian science into an advice column! Also she helped yours truly set some of the dates for the "History of Your Sex Appeal."

"I can see why people find the remoteness and yet the intimacy of the Internet enticing. I had a collaboration that started on the Internet. We wrote back and forth about a year before we actually met. He was rather surprised when he saw me. I was slouching about in shorts and a T-shirt. And we became very close in a lot of respects, and it was close in a way that would have been difficult, I think, if we had met in person first. He's quite shy. And I don't think it would have gotten beyond that. There were aspects of his personality that were very different from mine. But personal mannerisms are absent in an e-mail, and you can see below the surface to the real person."

So, here are the nine rules I've posted on the site (nothing like a little autoplagiarism to give tone to a chapter):

The Glorious Girls' "I Won't Suffer Fools Gladly" Guide to On-line Dating

#1. Put Up a Peachy Picture

Why do you think they gave Madam Curie the Nobel Prize? Because she *radiated*. So, gussy up. You can do the I'm-so-hip-I-shot-this-in-my-bathroom-mirror photo. Or, you can do what I call the Gilles Bensimon Special. (Gilles is the genius who creates and shoots the covers of *Elle*.) Hire a makeup artist. (I'm serious.—Why do you think cover girls *look* like cover girls?) Or visit the aforementioned makeup counter, have your hair blown out at a salon, don a man-murdering dress (or riding jacket and crème-caramel-colored, cashmere T-shirt, whatever your style), and ask a friend to spend the afternoon shooting you in different locales with various lighting (a pale pink sunset can make Ernest Borgnine look like Lara Flynn

Boyle). If Monsieur Bensimon rips through 20 rolls of film to get one perfect shot, why should *you*, a mere human, shoot less?[2]

#2. Create a Bewitching Screen Name

You're an enticing new lass on the World Wide Web (strike that . . . sounds *ancient*), you're the new girl on-line, and the name you create—a sobriquet that preserves your anonymity—will "brand" your image. One caution: unless you want to engage in sex sixty or seventy times a day with dozens of strapping young rakes, do NOT call yourself anything that smacks, ahem, of the bedroom, *viz*, Miss Behavin', The Naughty Professor, Boobalicious.

Titles/characters/poetic descriptions are excellent—"Lady-Chat-early," "HalleBerryTwin," and so on.

#3. Don't Write a Profile— Tell a Story

You're penning the opening chapter in what could turn out to be a big mesmerizing romance, so *come on*. "I like music, dogs, and hiking" (oh, the drama!) strangles your allure instead of heightening it. I adore this little "autobiography" written by a woman who recommended her ex on GreatBoyfriends.com:

---

2. Um, money?

Mad-flattering portraits can be made with a little pluck, a bit of right-brain intuition, one role of film, and a fabulous personal fantasy. If you possess a digital camera (or can borrow one), excellent! You can reel off 200 shots and chose the one with maximum charm.

I love behind-the-scenes of movies. I walked onto the set of Julia Roberts's new film, Mona Lisa Smile, *and the director, Mike Newell (a stranger to me), walked over and thanked me "for smiling at (him) so dimly." Made my week!*

Just three sentences, but anyone reading it will conclude that the writer is (A) eye-catching, (B) spontaneous, (C) bright, and (D) witty. The rule is, Don't tell 'em, show 'em.

#4. Spin & Spell

The I'm-just-a-little-mouse-turd-on-your-browser-so-I'm-going-to-bore-you-with-the-dumb-ass-truth approach is the twittiest mistake you can make. Roll your profile in gold dust, darling, and spin it like a ringed planet.

Love feeds on mystery AND honesty. Mystery keeps love eager, Honesty keeps love real. A wise woman never lies; but she knows how to make "reality" do cartwheels, as in this little example from a woman on the Web site:

I'd love to write something that will capture my personality and my zest for life—something that will make me stand out from the rest of the crowd—something creative and original, but instead, I'll just say:

I'm deep and complex with an inner fire that keeps me happy and motivated. I have a wonderful group of friends with whom I love spending time. I'm sociable, peppy, a tiny bit sassy, loving, sometimes funny, highly energetic, and intelligent (at least that's what I'm told!).

So, while I didn't pen an amazingly hysterical description of who I am, I think you get the picture.

Want another?

I'm an actress. I'm hot, yet dorky. I read. I tear up the dance floor when I'm not being a hermit. Everyone always picks me to be on their team nowadays. When I was younger, it was another story. But ever since I got the braces off, look out!

Both these women have taken care to be honest *and* engaging, and more important, their photos are absolute killers—elusive, thrilling, warm, sexy (the second woman appears to be wearing a *slip*! By Pan's hairy bollocks!)

#5. If Catherine the Great Could
Seduce Voltaire with Her Letters,
You Can Drop Men at Your Feet
with an E-Mail

When you see a fellow on the site that you fancy, drop him an e-mail. Something *short*. We've noticed the women who receive the most attention on our sites (aside from putting up intriguing photos) send

A. *brief*
B. *friendly*
C. *lighthearted*
D. *roguish*
E. *did I say brief?*

e-mails. Mention something that caught your attention in the guy's profile, something you have in common, something you disagree with, etc. Soon love letters (because this is what these e-mails *are*) will be whizzing around you like Eros' own hailstorm.[3]

A raucous courtship can begin with a sedate exchange about butterfly hunting . . . or end when "MrWallStreet" adds a P.S. begging to suck your kneecaps. You're writing the script, you're running the show. If you want a noble, true-blue guy, reveal (briefly!) valiant facets of your own character—add substance to style.

No need for Edith Wharton–grade cyclones of introspection—just a few comical/cynical/unclichéd insights about your day at work, or maybe how you're volunteering at the animal shelter. After three or four exchanges, if sparks are flying, you will move to "real" e-mail (off the site) and he'll ask for your number. I advise you to demur and, instead, ask him to give you *his* cell AND office numbers (just to keep him on the straight and narrow).

(*Note:* If you followed my advice in #1, your picture will cause men to bleat like goats and beg for an assignation right away. Hold off till you've exchanged *several* e-mails—ask him (casually) about his morning routine, where he went on his last vacation, what he thinks of his mother, and so forth—and then, after you converse on the phone, if you feel confident he's not a moron, you may condescend to appear in all your beauty and charm at Starbucks at 7 P.M.)

---

3. Just to snap the bra strap of this point one more time: We've discovered that women sending long e-mails (some of them running 1,500 words!) are less successful in finding romance. When they ask our advice, we show them how to shorten their notes down to 100 words or less (for the opening serve-and-volley). They always meet with greater success.

#6. Keep the First Rendezvous
Short & Safe

No matter how weak with excitement you are, no matter how much romantic tension is simmering just below the surface of your e-mails, NEVER agree to anything more than coffee (or drinks) at a café/museum/hot dog stand.

I don't have to whack you over the head with my Robert Clergerie black stretch boot and tell you to always meet in a public place, now do I, Doll? Or that you should Google him before planning a rendezvous to uncover any unadulterated facts? Or that you should tell your best friend when and where you're meeting him?

When you see him walk in, you will either feel a friendly (or interested) click in the first thirty seconds, or you won't, so do NOT waste time. The *average* man doesn't have a snowball's chance in hell of meeting your unattainable expectations anyway, so keep it short, keep it sweet. If, however, he walks in, and SWIIIIIIIP, your uterus wants to sail to Martinique with him, go on and have dinner.

#7. But If You're SERIOUSLY
Enamored, Do NOT Have Sex Until
You've Flogged His Trembling
Carcass into a State of Frenzy
Bordering on Insanity

If you think this could be It, wait. As Balzac says, "The duration of passion is proportional with the original resistance of the woman."

#8. However, If You're Using
Internet Dating for a Lusty
Romp . . .

Never in the history of the Ask Eeee column has any female ever been advised to stop enjoying incredible sex—and the array of queenhell sexual tastes presented on alt.com, for instance, are almost beyond comprehension. If you want a tryst (or several) and won't moan and cry afterward and act like a simp, go ahead. The same rules apply as in #6, with this addition: PROTECT YOUR-SELF, DARLING!

#9. Internet Dating Is Now Oh-So-
Cool It's Hip to Be Seen Doing It

Honey, if the newly wedlocked are jabbering in the august *New York Times* wedding pages about the "thrill" of meeting on-line, your coworkers and friends (not wanting to appear out of it) will think it's not only NOT geeky, but will think you're all the smarter and enchanting for doing it.

However, you must appear on an elite, thoroughbred site. In old E. Jean's opinion there are only four sites worthy of a top girl: Match.com (a magnificently broad array of choices), J-Date (if you're Jewish or want to date a Jewish prince, you can't beat this one), Spring Street Networks (these personals appear in several hip publications like *Jane, The New York Observer, New York*, and on Nerve.com and boast the most audaciously inventive members, many of whom are panty-hose models looking for hookups) . . . and GreatBoyfriends.com (the most trustworthy because women *vouch* for the men and we have the handsomest fellows in the world, swear to God—Cande and I personally throw all the losers off).

And now for the remaining 118 best places to meet the moneyed, the talented, the single, the handsome, the brave . . .

Wait. Wait. Before we begin, you should (*obviously*) pick the places *you* like. (E.g., you may sport more curves than Jeff Gordon's Chevy Monte Carlo, but revving your motor at a NASCAR event when you have no interest in stock cars is phonier than the air bags in Pam Anderson's chest.) It's best to have *something* in common with the man you are about to fall in love with.[4]

Also, I'm glancing through my notes here . . . I see some of the 118 "places" are not places, but ideas, or—well, I can't quite say what they are, they seem to be concepts, or fate-shakers, or maybe the blue sparks zigzagging off the Diamond of Destiny.

Sports

Suggestions for the Delectation of This Splendid Category

A. *Turn to the sports pages in today's paper.*

B. *Read the whole damn section. Do not skip the box scores.*

C. *Concentrate.*

D. *It's impossible to understand how men think unless you lock into their brain waves.*

---

4. And I'm not talking the "handsome, bronzelike Commemorative Tire Jack" from the Milwaukee Mile.

E. *Reading* every *single solitary detail about last night's NBA/ NFL/NHL/MLB games will expose the beasts' thought patterns and lay bare their primal lust for power, speed, carnage.*

F. *Now . . . if you continue to focus—I mean focus like a highly paid quarterback throwing a 47-yard pass to Jerry Rice— you'll lock onto the Male Brainscape and your own thought rhythms will change. You'll begin to see the routine events of your day as not routine, but as opportunities for "coming up big" and "scoring."*

G. *Hence, you will begin "thinking like a man."*

H. *Naturally, you do not care a flucking fartdoodle, no that's not a typo, what men think. (If you do not recall this principle, see Week One. See Week One at once!) No, you don't give one hot damn. But you now have the power to think like a man thinks, and this . . .*

I. *Gives you a diabolical, unsportsmanlike advantage.*

Shall we begin? Wait a minute. I don't have to tell you *where* to find the times and places for games and matches in the following categories do I? That's right. The sports section.

Sports Venues Where Men Always Outnumber Women

2. *Golf courses*
3. *Batting cages*
4. *Handball courts*

5. *Driving ranges*
6. *Squash courts*
7. *Gun clubs*
8. *Hockey rinks*
9. *Mountain bike trails*
10. *Rock-climbing establishments*
11. *Airfields/hang-gliding centers*
12. *Deep-sea diving resorts*

Let me interrupt here, may I? One of my ex-husbands and I vacationed on Bonaire—a hot little rock pile off the cost of Venezuela positively erupting with men, every one of them a diving fanatic. On the trip down, the plane was jammed with male divers—stockbrokers, doctors, lawyers, sales managers, professional football players, and so on.

Seated in the middle of the cabin were two women in their early thirties. Neither was particularly pretty, but both possessed an unthinkable amount of pizzazz. Twenty-five minutes out of New York they were toast of the plane.

They were trotting up and down the aisle, beaming with good humor, breaking into hearty laughter at the guys' jokes, introducing the football players to the cardiologists, finding everyone irresistible, burbling, erupting in explosions of delighted chortles—they were com*plete*ly the ringmistresses of the plane.

Now, I ask you, did either of these females so much as *own* a snorkel? No. But on Bonaire they were outnumbered by men twenty to one, their suitcases were filled with man-staggering swimsuits (we stayed at the same place so I had glimpses), and they played their womanly charms for all they were worth.

We were also on the same return flight, and again they were feted by the male passengers with everything but a ticker-tape parade. I managed to speak with them for a quick moment before we landed. They hadn't slept in 30 or 40 hours. Their hair was full of shells, one had somehow lost her shoes, but they looked like two bolts of lightning that had been searching for a place to strike—and had found it.

Where You'll Meet Flocks and Flocks of Men

Note: Montana's Madison River in September (i.e., fly-fishing season) is not on this list because even though men outnumber women fifty to one, I'd rather poke my eyes out with a bamboo pole than mention it because the happiest years of my life were lived in the "fly-fishing capital of the world," viz, Ennis, Montana, and when those East Coast, Ivy League morons arrived every September, I can say, without exaggeration, I'd never seen a bigger bunch of rich, line-tangling, trout-torturing assholes in my life.

13. *The U.S. Open (both golf and tennis)*
14. *Baseball spring training*
15. *The Super Bowl*
16. *The Masters*
17. *Formula One races*
18. *The Final Four*
19. *The Kentucky Derby*
20. *The Belmont Stakes*

Note from 2003: Spielberg and Capshaw, Parker and Broderick, Sigourney and Goldie, I could barely see Funny Cide lose the Triple Crown and my $1,000 through the fricking THRONGS of movie stars.

Note from 2002: Well . . . yes. I can personally recommend the Men's Room in the tony clubhouse section of Belmont Park fifteen minutes before War Emblem stumbles out of the gate, loses the Triple Crown, and my $200.

The facts:

There are about 80 emotionally intense women lined up to use the Ladies', so I dash into the Men's. EGADS! The poor buggers are so dumbstruck when I whirl in—alone, unescorted, wearing my Vivienne Westwood thoroughbred-blue suit and matching Chuck Taylor All Stars—nobody moves. It's a big place and smells like Secretariat's fundament. Ten or twelve statues of men are standing in front of the urinals. Then a rakish Black Jack Bouvier–type breaks the spell by exclaiming, "GIVE THIS YOUNG LADY A STALL, GENTLEMEN!"—whereupon the statues start moving and Jackie's father commences pounding on the stall doors.

"Thank you, sir," I say.

He all but drags some poor fellow out of the first compartment, and with a bow lower than a jockey's Jockeys he holds the door open for me.

Do you think I can, under these highly adventurous circumstances, actually relieve my bladder?

Ha!

However, as I leave (to a gentlemanly ovation!), several fellows follow me out to the champagne table to ask "which horse I have," and so on, and one rogue wants to meet me later in the paddock.

21. *The Rose/Orange/Sugar Bowls (or any big-time college game)*

22. *The glamour events at the Olympics (or, now that I think of it, the nonglam events might be better—cycling, kayaking, etc.)*

23. *Title fights*

The big title fights bring *hailstorms* of men. The prefight Showtime or HBO parties are wall-to-wall movie stars, rap stars, basketball stars, Olympic stars, directors, Oscar winners, etc. If you're near ringside, you'll have Denzel at your left elbow and Jack at your right. Indeed, the last time I went to a title fight, I could imagine the headlines:

Journalist Discovered in MGM Grand Hotel Room
Undergarments Cut Off Blood to
Writer's Cerebral Cortex

Fashionable Elle *boxing reporter E. Jean Carroll was found half-dead late last evening in her hotel room.*

Carroll, who traveled from New York to Las Vegas for the heavyweight championship bout, had been seen early in the afternoon running around the HBO Arena shrieking excitedly, "I've never seen so many men in my life! This is a Cojónes Carnival! This is a Phallic Field Day!"

Frantic Emergency Medical workers and two Las Vegas SWAT teams took 47 minutes to extricate Carroll from her panty girdles.

When reached for comment at the Nevada State Hospital where she is recovering, Carroll, who was eating a box of DoveBars, said she wore the girdles "because the sport of boxing is obviously so weight-crazed.

"Heck," said Carroll, laughing, "not even a deranged MODEL could come up with something as wacky as 'flyweight, bantamweight, featherweight, and welterweight.'"

Earlier in the evening police received multiple reports that Carroll was "bothering" and "pestering" Shaquille O'Neal at the HBO party. Brad Pitt, Pierce Brosnan, Justin

Timberlake, and Tiger Woods have all denied rumors Carroll
was trying to make out with them.

Off-Beat Sports Events Where You're Sure to Meet Even More Fellows, but If You're a Snotty Woman with No Sense of Humor, You Won't Like Any of Them, So Don't Waste Your Time

24. *Motocross championships*
25. *The quarter-horse races at Ruidoso, New Mexico*
26. *The Indianapolis 500*
27. *Daytona 500*
28. *Any NASCAR race*

I know, I know, I kinda did No. 26, No. 27, and No. 28 but my iMac has taken on a life of its own (it crashes whenever I write the words "My pit bull is a living deity"), and I can't figure out how to renumber everything.

29. *Professional wrestling matches (best when there's a big pay-*
per-view heavyweight championship on the line)
30. *Cheyenne Frontier Days*
31. *Any small-town rodeo in Colorado, Idaho, Utah, Wyoming,*
or Montana
32. *The Laconia (New Hampshire) Motorcycle Rally*
33. *The Sturgis (South Dakota) Rally (500,000 Harley riders)*

All women of the highest caliber have a bit of biker babe in their blood.

34. *The Burning Man Festival in the Nevada desert*

It's artistic, it's spiritual, it's bizarre (bring your own food, water, shelter), it's big (25,000 people), but lately it's being overrun with Hollywood types—actors, agents, writers, etc.

Sports Places I Can't Wedge into the Other Sections

35. *While you're waiting for You Know Who in his shining armor to come along and idolize your finest attributes, go scout the tents, racquets, skates, running shoes, croquet sets, basketballs, and Swiss army knives in an upscale sports equipment store.*

An LA acquaintance of mine (a rambunctious and playful casting director) says she's been asked out by a cute guy every single time she shops for camping equipment.

36. *You may feel profound ambivalence about this suggestion, but if you're in the right mood, and a championship series/play-off/wild card game is on TV, don your trademark—you do have a trademark, Doll, don't you? An outfit you know you look good in—and go watch it at a sports bar.*

In Hyde Park, New York, just across the road from FDR's home there's a small brewery with a sports bar. I don't know the name of this depraved groggery, but I spent one of the most flagrant, electrifying hours of my life there.

My friend Marsha Pinkstaff and I had been at FDR's house

reading his love letters to Eleanor and had just hauled our shanks onto stools at the end of the bar to watch the Kentucky Derby, when a burst of filthy thunder assaulted our ears. We looked out the window and saw The Menace. A couple of big, evil-looking guys on monster Harleys. Now, Marsha Pinkstaff is, without question, the biggest snob in New York. She is beautiful, imperious, and is very, very, very cruel to men.

At the sight of the outlaws, she turned her chin up in the air and went back to watching Jim McKay and Charlsie Canty doing the prerace buildup on the monitor above the bar. But suddenly there he was: Manly Man. (Marsha later called his abrupt appearance in the doorway "the entrance of the Blue-Collar Machismo.")

Actually both motorcycle rogues were quite handsome, but Marsha's man (their attraction was so instantaneous, he immediately became "Marsha's Man") was extraordinary. Tan, startling blue eyes, a powerful build soooo NOT chiseled in the gym, extremely dramatic hands, like God's own fingers on the Sistine Chapel where He's making the big mistake of creating Adam first. In fact, I whispered to Marsha, "I'll bet he's an artist." She didn't hear me. His macho beauty had annihilated her hearing.

The two men sat down directly opposite us, about 18 feet away, exactly under the television in Marsha's line of sight.

The race started.

Everybody in the bar was glued to the various screens and starting to yell, but Marsha never took her eyes off her outlaw's face. Nor did he shift his gaze from her. The race was a stunner, and the shouting and whooping and stamping and pounding as War Emblem streaked to the head of the field was deafening. (Yes, the same horse from the Belmont—the Derby is the first leg of the Triple Crown.) But Marsha's Man never moved. He held a glass of brandy and lasered his eyes into hers. The air between them vibrated. Miss

Marsha Pinkstaff was his goddess. Miss Marsha Pinkstaff was his nymph. Miss Marsha Pinkstaff was adored. Miss Marsha Pinkstaff was within one bat of an eyelash from being thrown on the floor and snogged and boffed till her brains fell out.

After the race was over, I got so excited watching Marsha's Man looking at her, I forgot I'd been a vegetarian for the last 22 years and ordered a bloody cheeseburger! Anyway, by this time, some local talent was hitting on "my" outlaw, so I had nothing to do with myself.

And the end of this little love story?

"I'm going over there," I said.

"No!" said Marsha.

"I want to ask if he's a famous sculptor."

"No!"

"I'm going."

"Please don't."

"Yes."

"No."

"I'm going."

"You're not going."

"I'm just going to ask if he's the famous Hyde Park sculptor."

"Sit down!"

In the end she forbade me. She's my best friend. I did as she asked. I've regretted it ever since. The reason she didn't want me to go was so stupid! So wimpy. So cluckish. She was wearing lightly tinted sunglasses because her right (or left) eye was tearing a little from an allergy and she didn't feel she looked her best. That was the reason. Now, Marsha Pinkstaff not looking her best is about twelve times better-looking than anybody else (indeed, sometime in the last century, after bribing several judges, the bat-lashing Butler University sophomore beat me for the title of Miss Indiana). Stupid. Stupid. Stupid.

To this day, we argue about "Marsha's Man"—me maintaining I should have stepped in and introduced them, thereby forcing her to "seize the moment"; and Marsha contending that it was "a perfect moment unspoiled."

"You don't fool around with perfect moments," she says. "Now he can live forever in my fantasies."

"On the other hand," I always say, with a snort, "you could be living with *him* forever."

Sports Strategies That Will Bring You Personal Triumph as Well as a Multitude of Admirers

37. *Look here, Doll, you want a madcap season? Join your company's (or your church's or neighborhood saloon's) mixed softball (volleyball, basketball, bowling) league. 100% fun guaranteed, plus beers afterward with the scoundrels and aces of the opposing team.*

38. *Reserve a tennis court at your local park for this Sunday. Arrive without a partner. There will be several guys (who, naturally, didn't sign up) waiting for a court. (This is particularly true for New York's Central Park.) Or appear at your scheduled time with a girlfriend and suggest mixed doubles with the lads-in-waiting.*

39. *Play golf, for godsakes! Handball! Racquetball! Take up skeet shooting! Parachuting! Hang gliding! Mountain biking! Bull riding! Rock climbing! Scuba diving! Enough exclamation points! Criminey!*

40. *Now, I know you're a big-time, big-money career woman, but deep inside you have a soul, and your soul is a little girl who wants to play badminton. Set up a net with your girlfriends in the park near the softball fields/basketball/tennis courts. (A badminton set complete with net, shuttlecocks, and four rackets runs about $40 at Target.) Open your cooler. It is full of ice and Sam Adams. Wear shorts. Start playing. Soon fellows will be begging to join.*

(I've caught flack for that suggestion, but . . . *come on*. Your future can only be intriguing if you have the guts to be intriguing. And if that means batting around a birdie and striking a blow against sitting at home, then all right.)

41. *Yacht clubs/marinas/sailing clubs—if you don't know anyone who owns a boat, call up/drop by and offer to help crew.*

42. *Aspen. Vail. December. Rich assholes in fur coats. Crested Butte, Tahoe, Alta, Park City, Telluride—January. February. March. Cowboys and cool guys in such high concentrations as to become actually lethal.*

43. *Frisbee. Now, Sweetie, please. If you don't run to the park this very moment and hit a man in the back of the head with your dog's Frisbee, I'm going to refuse to speak to you.*

44. *If you are a mother with young children, volunteer to help at swim meets, soccer games, Little League, etc. These are prime places to meet single fathers (and women who know single fathers).*

My neighbor Andrea, a divorced therapist with two little kids, was introduced to a lovely fellow by a woman she met at her child's gymnastics class a couple of weeks ago; and yesterday Andrea came screeching to a skidding halt in front of my cottage, leaned out her Jeep window, and yelled for me to come with her to look at wedding dresses, swear to God.

45. *Roller-skate to work.*

46. *Ditto scooter.*

47. *Ditto moped.*

48. *Ditto bike.*

(It's impossible for chaps to succumb to your manifold charms unless they *see* you. No.'s 45, 46, 47, and 48 put you outside. Plus, these modes of transport have an exhilarating, purifying effect and you will arrive at work with fresh ideas.)

49. *Forget polo. Too many high-grade bitches. Of course, if you, yourself, are a high-grade bitch . . . enjoy!*

50. *You're in the park, right? You're at the field, the grounds, the court, correct? Upon the conclusion of the rugby match (cricket, lacrosse, soccer), stroll up to the nerviest, cunningest player, smile, and hand him a cold beer from your bag.*

The Street

Ok. Ok. I take that back about the Internet and sports events being the best places to meet the male beast (did I say that, or was I just thinking it?). The street is a damned delightful place too. This is the one where you're walking down to the corner to pick up *The Economist,* and you grab that old whore Fate by the ankle bracelet and vow, "By God, from this moment on, I'm cutting myself a swath!"

In other words, you're going to do what Marsha Pinkstaff did not do:

51. *Seize the moment!*

Moments occur as you run around living your life. *Viz*, on the walk to Wing Sun's Dry Cleaners on South Main, when you see a man and there's a flash of recognition . . . you've never laid eyes on him before, but you seem to *know* each other[5] . . . instead of letting him pass, instead of glancing down at the pavement, instead of years from now looking back on your life and wondering why you never found your "true love," instead, instead, instead . . . look him in the eye and smile.

It may turn out to be nothing but a three-second saucy intrigue, but why should your future existence be at the mercy of not giving in to an impulse?

Friends

52. *Work the phones. Call everyone you know and, in the spirit of 100% (endearing) candor, ask them to fix you up.*

53. *You've heard all the ladies' mag stuff about giving parties and asking your friends to bring eligible men. Uh-unh. You should hold a regular poker night with the boys.*

---

5. I can't prove it, but I think your DNA is reading his DNA, and the sudden jolt you feel is Ma Nature telling you, WHOA!

54. *Pull a Peggy Siegal. The slender, dark-haired Manhattan public relations maven (with an acclaimed wardrobe) told her friends she'd give a new Mercedes-Benz to the first person to find her a man.*

Not a bad idea. But the smarter move would have been to offer a Mercedes to anyone who'd keep men AWAY from her. It would have made Peggy irresistible.[6]

Speaking of Which . . .

55. *If you live in a city of over 200,000 and can afford $2,000 a month, hire a PR agent. He/she will arrange for you to be invited to the parties, introduce you to posh people, get your name in the papers, turn you into a socially huge phenomenon with appropriate hangers-on, and generally push you over the edge so every man in town sees you "properly amplified."*

Work

56. *I've said it a thousand times. One of the main reasons for going to work is to get involved with your co-workers. Where else are attractive persons of all ages and both sexes thrown together in seductive struggles for money and power two thousand hours a year? What other locale allows you daily,*

---

6. She is still single.

repeated, incessant, perpetual chances to fall in love and get paid for it?

The Gym

57. *Best of Irish luck diverting the attention of anybody in the forbiddingly crowded and sweaty Monday/Tuesday-night time frames. Instead, work out on Friday and Saturday nights. You'll be glowing when you meet friends at ten-thirty at Balthazar.*

My friend Helen Marien, the New York handbag designer, is a former personal trainer and she says:

"I can tell you the health club is an excellent place to find a man. BUT a woman should not go on overcrowded Monday nights when everyone goes (guilt-ridden after weekends), nor Tuesday. Wednesday and especially Thursday and Friday nights are the best. That's when the only members who come in are the committed ones (to their health anyway). They are earnest, physically fit men. Everyone else is out doing the club scene—including all the young women!"

Dogs

58. *Adopt a dog from the ASPCA, Petfinders.com, or your local shelter. Walk the dog four times a day, and your chances for a romantic encounter shoot up to 28 times a week. Twenty-eight chances to meet someone divine! Now. You are a ca-*

*reer woman? You do not possess a grotesque amount of time
to "beat the bushes" for a man? A dog is the solution.*

And if you're not walking that dog past the Porsche dealerships,
basketball courts, medical centers, and fire stations, I'm going to
give you a flea bath.

As a matter of fact, the other night I was driving up Riverside
Drive in New York and kept seeing men—some of them damn good-
looking—with dogs. I was so struck, I stopped and looked at my
watch. Eleven. Men, straight men, with dogs were bloody EVERY-
WHERE between 73rd and 110th. Riverside Park looked like the
Canine Unit of the U.S. army. And not a female in sight. (My guess
is women don't want to walk in the park at night.)

The editor of this fine book, Mr. David Hirshey, has Fred, a gigantic imbecile of a rescued retriever, the color of Cheez Doodles,
who shoves (shoves!) David out of bed every morning at 6 A.M. so he
can sleep with Miss S. Squire, David's shapely wife.

Now, I posit that a woman, even a small woman, even a very
small woman, even half an Olsen twin, could walk naked through
Riverside Park at night with Fred and not only *not* be hassled . . . but
would meet some lovely, honest, nonmanipulative men—nonmanipulative because these are men walking their dogs instead of sitting in
a bar telling lies to women.

Get a dog! You'll enjoy sleeping with the only creature on earth
who will love you more than it loves itself.

Art

59. *You know this: gallery openings, estate sales, art museums,
blah, blah, blah. Go, but please, none of your I'm-so-arty-I-*

can-only-wear-black, no, no, no, no, no, no, no, no. The idea is to look like a brilliant artwork, not a worn-out stub of charcoal.

60. *Set up your easel in the park, even if you can paint only abstract smudges. Inspire curiosity.*

61. *Poetry readings in cafés are excellent, particularly if you are the poet.*

My extremely happily married friend, the poet Marilyn Johnson, who met her husband, Rob Fleder, when they were both editors at *Esquire*, wears a see-through Cosmic Pink shirt at her readings.

62. *Poetry slams are good places to meet mercurial, heart-ripe young Chris Carrabba types.*

63. *Don't forget film festivals.*

Music

64. *The other day on* The Early Show *on CBS Bonnie Raitt was asked why she had taken up guitar. Her answer: "Because it was a cool way to meet guys." The National Guitar Workshop (which has sites all over the country) holds seminars for jazz, pop, classical guitarists, etc. I've never been, but I hear it's 90% men.*

65. *If you have a dress . . . the opening night of opera season. (You will meet a nice gay man and HE will fix you up with his straight friends.)*

66. *Any concert in the park. Many music lovers pack complicated five-course meals into wicker receptacles replete with the droll*

*linens they've brought back from Aix-en-Provence. You bring
Budweiser and hot dogs. Men of Taste will run from all directions and fall upon your basket like starving badgers.*

67. *Form your own band. Start playing clubs. Why not? Can't
the hopes of a generation surge through YOU as well as
through Eve's life buoy–sized buttocks?*

68. *Music festivals. My friend, Sarah Lazin, the literary agent,
says, "The New Orleans JazzFest is huge and cruisy. There are
forty thousand to seventy thousand people who go on any given
day, and many, many of them are single. Also there are hunky-
looking guys with women who could use immediate makeovers,
but that's another book—shows you don't have to be beautiful.
And if you hang out where the guys are (i.e., the Blues Tent), it's
impossible NOT to meet a man. There are other music festivals
across the U.S., and also internationally, but JazzFest is the
daddy of them all—two four-day weekends of great music on
the racetrack, with the intervening week filled with music in all
the fabled legendary clubs of New Orleans."*

Churches, Synagogues, Professional Organizations, Causes—Especially Animal Rights, Save-the-Jungle/River/Mountain, Political Campaigns, Yadda, Yadda, Yadda

69. *All come highly recommended by my friends, and I can
vouch for the best-looking men in Montana working for the
Nature Conservancy, Sierra Club, etc., etc. As for church . . .
the very lovely Sarah Lazin (again) says, "I'm sure there are*

ways of meeting guys all over the U.S. no matter what your religion, but in New York City, Friday-night Shabbat services at B'nai Jeshurun are known as the singles services and several thousand people cram into the church each week. (It has to be held at a church, since the synagogue is too small to fit everyone in!)"

70. *Join your city's Junior League. Terribly snotty, but these women do some decent charity work, they've opened up to become more inclusive, and they know* all *the rich eligible men.*

Drinking, Smoking, Eating

71. *Met my first husband, Steve, at a nightclub in Chicago. (Actually, we had gone to school together, and he's a great, funny, magnetic guy and is now editor in chief of his own imprint at National Geographic.) Met my second husband, John, the aforementioned anchorman, at Elaine's in New York.*

72. *Meeting friends for dinner at a prestige restaurant is expensive, but Ok. Meeting friends at the last minute for interesting $12 litchi martinis at seven-thirty at the bar in Citarella is* better *than Ok. It's sexy, and if you order five baskets of french fries, it's dinner with a delicious lack of stress. Thank you, George Bush. Your recession has created a popular new way to meet men—an evening out over cocktails at the bars and lounges of hip restaurants.*

73. *Tasting parties sponsored by wine shops and vineyards can turn out to be more amusing than the Lucy grape-stomping scene.*

NOTE: Now that smoking is banned everywhere but your own personal bathroom, the sidewalks *in front* of elite bars and restaurants are generating wonderfully ditzy preemptive-strike-type Meet-Cutes.

Cars

74. *The single most vital material possession of a Man Catcher (after a thrilling wardrobe) is a sweet ride. I'll brook no argument about this. The car has always been the ultimate American dream machine—it's an image, a fantasy, an identity. I don't need to go into how cars are a really, really giant deal with men, now do I? Buy a classic car and drive it. By classic I mean anything older than 1984 or less than $900. The chaps cannot keep their hands off an old '67 Dodge Cornet. (Too bad they don't feel the same about old women.)*

A '66, butter-yellow Cadillac convertible sits in yours truly's driveway because yours truly was absolutely forced to stop driving it in Manhattan because guys would fling themselves on the hood at stoplights and wish to engage yours truly in long conversations about "What year is this beauty?" and so on. Yours truly also must invest about $12,000 to get said Caddy out of said driveway after sitting so long.

75. *Car shows are good. So are boat shows, come to think of it.*

Mano a Mano

76. *Cigar bars. Dress: unsettling. Open-toed, open-heeled, open-arched shoes tied on with black ribbons. Short cocktail frock. Awed crowds will form.*

77. *Pool halls*

   Dress: as above.

78. *Any army post, air force, marine, or navy base*

After nine weeks following young Jersey girl Tonya Bey through basic training for CBS at Fort Leonard Wood, Missouri, I highly (oh, quite, quite highly) recommend army posts.

NOTE: Don't worry about getting on the post—the clubs, restaurants, and sports bars just outside the gates are swarming with sergeant majors, lieutenants, captains, coloniels.

The Man Trip

79. *Grab a friend, load up the car, roll back the roof, throw a kiss to the local lads, and hit every burg between Clarence, New York, and Maxwell, California, named after a man . . . or if you prefer . . . every town between Craig, Colorado, and Pierre, South Dakota . . . or between Stevens Point, Wisconsin, and Vernon, Texas, etc. (Well, you can't very well visit every town named after a man—there are at least 200 places named after former presidents alone.)*

If you do it right and stop by the baseball game in Gary, Indiana, and the Firemen's Breakfast in Hannibal, Missouri, you won't even make it to wherever you were heading. You'll be engaged to three different men before you hit Cecil, Pennsylvania.

Guys You Already Know and Wish to Turn into Your Own Personal Male Concubines

80. *If there's a man of your acquaintance who gives you a sharp ping of pleasure every time you see him (but you sort of remain anonymous or invisible to him), then "run into" the unsuspecting bugger at the next Cubs game. Send an amorous shock down his spine by not appearing as he's accustomed to seeing you appear. Viz, if he always sees you in tight, black bull-fighting pants, gauze blouse, and chiffon Kangol cap, then show up at Wrigley Field in a suit so prim and civilized, the umpire stops the inning and orders both teams to bow in your direction.*

That will stir things up. And when things are stirred up? A Man Catcher succeeds.

Ideas/Places I Didn't Think of, Though Luckily My Girlfriends Did

81. *The Appalachian Mountain Club*

Christy Marshuetz: *The AMC has a chapter in most states, and the men are yummy! Fit, outdoorsy types. I'm a 31-year-old assistant professor at Yale, and pitifully*

*still single, so maybe you should take this suggestion
with a grain of salt.*

Kara DiCamillo (Kara is a self-employed public relations professional): *I'm a member of the Connecticut
chapter. I've been on several hikes (there's one just about
every weekend all year round), and they also have bike
rides, kayaking, etc. It's a great place to meet men because
you already share a common interest. The best thing
about going on these social hikes, etc., is that everyone
WANTS to be there and everyone is so friendly!*

82. *Habitat for Humanity*

Brenda Ellis (Brenda owns a business that provides
sentencing support to criminal defense attorneys. She
enthusiastically recommends scuba diving and under-
water photography and adds the following): *Certain volunteer efforts lead to meeting men. Politics, especially
fund-raising, but not party-planning. And Habitat for
Humanity is great, or Christmas in July, or any short-
term construction project.*

83. *Geek meets*

Amyjane Schrader (Amyjane is a programmer for Mi-
crosoft, which is how she discovered "the untapped sea of
geeky boys"): *Quake parties, software releases, hardware
swap meets, openings of electronic stores. Many benefits!*

A. *Not too many women there—if any (besides you).*
B. *There's a pretty good chance the men will be intelli-
gent.*
C. *Since you're there, they'll suspect you're smart too.*

D. *Geeky guys don't grow up with women throwing them-selves at them—this makes them respectful and honest.*
E. *Most have great jobs AND they are loaded.*

84. *The Rainy Day Umbrella Maneuver*

Marian Pereira (a corporate marketer who likes poetry slams—Marian is the one who vouched for #66—and Flemish art): *When there's a downpour, find a handsome guy with a large umbrella, scoop in under it, and say, "I'm going a few blocks, can you give me a ride?" I've done it and it works.*

85. *Home Depot*

Ms. Sterling Odom (currently studying for her MBA at Carnegie Mellon; also volunteers as a mentor to female inmates in prison and says prison is NOT a place to meet men): *Any big home-improvement store is good. My favorite strategy is to ask a perfect, broad-shouldered male where the "naval jelly" is. He's always so impressed that I know this product is for rust removal and not an accessory to foreplay.*

86. *Airports*

Jennifer Wills (a buyer for a department store): *I've met two of my past boyfriends while waiting to catch a flight; and I met my current beau and Love of My Life at the baggage terminal in a foreign airport.*

87. *Sign-up boards in parks*

Kate Brame (a strategy—you can say that again!—ana-lyst for an investment bank): *Central Park has a board full of names of people who are looking for tennis partners. The names are color-coded by beginner/intermediate/ advanced. All you have to do is decide which category you fall into and write down the names/numbers (preferably those of the opposite sex), call them, and see if they'd like to play!*

(Yes, this was mentioned earlier, but I thought it was so charming, I wanted to note it again.)

88. Join AA

Candice (Candice recently bid melodious adieu to Silicon Valley and now lives on the East Coast): *I've gotten on the sober track and have noticed some interesting men at the gatherings. I look forward to meeting someone with the same mind-set as mine. It's a different tack, but as much as I want to meet a great guy, I want someone nice and lasting. Not flashy/flash in the pan.*

By the way, my friend just met the best guy in her new church group. She joined with strictly spiritual intentions, but lucky her! She's landed a very sweet guy in the process.

89. Get yourself on the board of an organization

Marilyn Johnson the poet (again): *I know a widower of some means who met his second wife serving on a hospital board. My Writer's Center Board has an interesting mix of married and the newly divorced. Plus, usually if you serve on a board, you're rich.*

90. *Always talk to strangers on the train*

Amy Knoll: *My dear friend, let's call her "K," met her man on the PATH train from Jersey City to New York. He was with a group of young men and kept looking at K and smiling a sad, wan smile. K was intrigued.*

Soon he sidled over to her somewhat shakily, but still smiling. The train was swaying from side to side. He stumbled and sat down next to her. After initial pleasantries, K inquired where the man was going.

"Going out," he said.

He was clearly drunk. His breath smelled of alcohol even though it was barely past noon on a Saturday.

"Well," K ventured, "are you really sure that's a good idea? It seems you've had quite a good time already."

"Yes," he said, "I must go out. I'm really depressed."

K peered at him sternly over her Jackie O dark glasses, looking straight into his eyes.

"Why are you so depressed?"

"Well," he said, "my dad has cancer, my mom died, my brother died, and my other brother's an asshole."

Some pickup line.

When the train came to a stop, the young man's friends got up to leave and held the door for him. "Come on! This is our stop!"

"But I'm trying to talk to the pretty lady," he slurred.

So K, ever the efficient corporate lawyer, handed him her business card. "What the hell?" she thought. "This guy will never call anyway."

But he did. He called the next day completely em-

barrassed and took her out to dinner. He was a nice man, a contractor who was nursing his sick father and kept a house in the country. They were married the next year and are now awaiting a baby boy.

91. *Bagel places at 8 A.M. on any random Sunday*

Christina Consolé (Christina adores everything French and is, of course, in fashion): *They come in to get their pregolf fare, dahlink! I've met a few charmers this way.*

92. *Karaoke bars*

Francis Baker: *I'm no songbird (I work in investments!), but I was having a blast singing a Madonna tune. A really wonderful guy came up to me and complimented my performance. We ended up having a very nice relationship.*

93. *The software, science fiction, and business sections of bookstores*

Kim Watts: *These are hotbeds. I know, I'm an executive editor of a national magazine. I've spotted cuties but, alas, never knew how to approach or let myself be approached.*

94. *Never judge a book by its etc., etc.*

Kimberly Kirkendall (owner of a management consulting firm): *While parking my car at a restaurant, the valet starting talking to me. He wouldn't give up! Even when a couple of handsome lawyers joined me. While we were waiting for our table a friend of mine had a per-*

sonal emergency, and I had to rush out. When the valet handed me the keys, I put my business card in his pocket (but no tip). He was handsome, direct, and he called the next morning. Turns out he owns the valet business and was filling in for someone. He's national sales manager for a biotech firm. We've dated for almost a year.

95. *Cooking class*

Damiana Vance (pursuing a culinary arts career): *My latest interest is a man who helped rescue my sheet pan of biscotti from crashing to the floor in pastry class. We've only been on one date so far, so I'm not picking out china. But we've set our second date for this coming weekend. Crossed fingers!*

96. *Acts of God*

Kristi Walker (Kristi is vice president of client services for a software company; and as her personal trainer is staying for a couple of weeks in her guest room, Kristi is being forced to sneak pizza): *I was living in San Francisco when the '89 earthquake hit. I was home alone watching the World Series. My area was hit particularly hard. I ran outside to see if I could help and started talking to this guy. Turns out he lived in Berkeley and had no way of getting home. After determining he was "normal," I invited him over. We ended up playing Trivial Pursuit by candlelight. He then had to leave to go to his hospital. (He was a doctor.)*

I didn't think I'd see him again. It was such a horrible event that it seemed inappropriate to even think of a "date." But he showed up on my doorstep the next day with champagne and roses! We dated for two years and are still great friends.

97. *Buy him a martini*

Robynn Ferguson (a surgical nurse): *When you're enjoying a happy hour cocktail, and there's a gorgeous guy at the end of the bar loosening his tie, send him a drink via the bartender.*

98. *Feed your local engine company*

Yinka Abdurrahman (Yinka is an "ex-geek" who now makes and markets skin creams . . . "Moisturizer handmade from scratch; gnarly skin is never in"): *Show up with a basket of cookies/goodies for your neighborhood fire department.*

99. *Medical center cafeteria*

Cindy Diakow (an event planner): *Lots of hotties in surgical. Made some great friends.*

100. *Let your friend find you Mr. Dazzling*

Jennifer Williamson (just graduated from law school—"Hopefully I'll be a lawyer when bar exam results come out!"): *Jessica, my friend, has this 10-year habit of finding me men by identifying the best-looking one around and literally calling them over—as in, "Hey, you coming out of the Porta Potti!" She then proceeds to introduce me to him. It's always embarrassing but effective. I've met several boyfriends this way! Her success rate is 100%!*

The last occasion was at a wine-and-polo weekend.

The guy was a sales executive and former model named Bill. He was HOT. He ended up ditching his friends and hanging out with us. He stayed with me in my hotel that night and we went to the polo match the next day. As it turned out, I lost my plane ticket—not on purpose, I swear—so we spent not only my remaining time together, but an entire week!

Then he visited me in San Diego two weeks later. I returned to the East Coast to go to his sister's wedding two weeks after that and met his family. We dated seriously for two years!

101. *When you got it, flaunt it*

Marianne Segashes (a computer consultant who loves France, photography, champagne, five-star hotels, and 300 thread counts): *You know how you always feel like a million bucks after you get your hair cut and styled and everyone stares at you because you're feeling beautiful "within"?*

I make sure I have a few hours free after I get my hair done to go out and around. I meet men everywhere. Mostly I've noticed that men react to what I'm feeling inside. If I'm feeling beautiful and sexy, that's what I exude. So it's not the locale, it's what's going on inside me. I'm part French, so I never go out as a frump because I know the man of my dreams can be ANYWHERE, even at the gas station.

102. *Admire his car*

Jennifer Paquette (writer): *This may come across as a bit egotistical, but I have absolutely no problem meeting*

men. *I met my current "on and off" at the Beverly Con-*
nection parking garage. I was eyeing his Aston.

103. *Take up home brewing*

Julianne Gebhard (Julianne is senior application devel-
oper for an e-commerce site; she volunteers as a crisis
counselor for rape victims): *It helps if you actually* like
beer. The home-brew supply places are crawling with
men, as are the beer fests. These are connoisseurs, not a
bunch of drunk frat boys throwing up around a keg. I'm
always surprised to be one of the few women at these
events. And if you don't like beer, it could be because you
haven't tried all the different varieties.

104. *Buy two tickets to the theater, the symphony, the museum*

Julianne (again): *I'm a single woman and make a fair*
amount of money. I often find there's a show I'd like to
see, but don't always have a date. I've started purchasing
two tickets to whatever I want to go to, and then when I
meet some interesting man, I invite him along.

Because I do volunteer counseling of rape victims in
the ER, I get mounds and mounds of invitations to charity
events and I always meet someone interesting. Or some-
times I just go with girlfriends—especially those who try to
make ends meet on the paltry amount of money that's paid
to teachers and social workers, and afterward we go to
some downtown martini bar in our little black dresses.

105. *Ski lifts*

Ignacia de Pano (Ignacia is a lawyer from Barcelona
who sent this note from a beautiful little Mediterranean

village by the sea): *A wonderful place to meet men is waiting at a ski lift. The more difficult the slope, the better. The line is always full of nice-looking men and very few women. Then you take the tele-chair together, and while you're in the air, you get to know each other. He can't go away!*

106. *Seduce a guy at work*

Martha (does not wish her last name used because she works with a heart-lung machine [keeps people alive during bypass surgery] company and advises everyone to "have no heart attacks anytime soon please, because there are lots of 'quality' issues"): *I'd been working for about nine months with FH (Future Husband). We'd been pals, going out in groups and hanging around. I fixed him up with a few single women and he listened to me whine about the three-month relationships I seemed to be the master of.*

One night a bunch of us went out to a bar/pool hall in downtown Denver, very upscale and yuppie—I'd recently been dumped, and here I was again, talking to morons in a bar that I was way too old to be in. So this one fellow is chewing my ear off about how great he is, while I'm frantically gulping down my chardonnay, and I see FH across the room looking as miserable as I was feeling. I start jumping up and down, waving to get his attention, anything to get away from Moron Man Who Loves Himself Too Much, and FH comes over. Perfect excuse to excuse myself. I asked him if there was any chance he was ready to leave, and he said he was so ready to leave!

So I suggest we go for a swim at my place. When we

get there, I slip on my suit and off we go to climb over the fence (avec more alcohol! Quelle horreur!). I jump in the pool and watch FH strip down to his white Calvin Klein boy's briefs—hang on, need to collect my thoughts after remembering that one—cyclist body and all—okay, I'm back.

As we're swimming around and having fun, for the life of me I can't figure out why he isn't trying to kiss me. So I ask him, "Mind if I kiss you just once?" FH nods the affirmative and I kiss him. After a marathon of kissing, absolutely no touching, he's still hanging around and says to me, "Well I can't wait forever to catch you between boyfriends." After that, he never went home. Last Monday was our two-year celebration of that evening, and in less than two months we're getting married!

107. *The Seattle Speedway*

Cathy Robertson: *I have an idea for meeting men and it had never occurred to me before even though it's so totally obvious. I am married, though not blind, and I work for an tax and accounting firm in Washington State. I took my first trip to SIS (Seattle International Speedway) for some big race with a bunch of famous drivers in it. I am telling you, I was totally and completely surrounded by men men men. Everywhere I turned there was a good-looking guy within reach, and I made a mental vow to take my best single friend there next time she visits. The best thing about it was that besides the fact that there were so many good-looking guys around, they were all acting like themselves, in an area that they felt comfortable in, and so you could easily see what type of person they were. If I'd been single, I would've jumped at the chance to walk right up to one of those hunks, summon interest in the sport, and ask questions. So much easier than meeting some dork in a bar!*

(NOTE: We will not hear about car racing ever, ever again in *M.R.R.N.* So, take a last look at Miss Cathy's idea now.)

108. *Sit on the dock of the marina*

Diana Richards (a sales professional, lives in Southern California): *The best place to meet men, California style, is to go where they keep their boats—the marinas. Also Landmark Meetings. Has this hit the East Coast yet? It's the new version of est for those touchy-feely men.*

109. *Internet parties*

Jen Diebel (starting an on-line networking business called NetWorkNetPlay): *I was single until I was 32, so I tried all the ways to meet men—church, expensive matchmaking services, blind dates, personal ads, telepersonals, hanging out at the apartment pool, friends' parties, etc. Some worked, some did not, mostly not.*

Then I tried the Internet. Like most single girls I had a list of "criteria" that men needed to meet in order to even be considered. In my selections, I always seemed to end up with very similar people—engineers, accountants, or other similar straightforward, safe, secure-type men. They were all nice enough but not necessarily right. Along the way I weeded out those who didn't seem to be what I was looking for.

As it turns out, my current husband (of three years) was one of those "deletes." In fact, I "deleted" him four or five times. My reasons: he was too young (eight years my junior to be exact—three years pushed the envelope for me), he didn't have a picture, and he just didn't get into enough detail in his profile.

Fast-forward past the "deletes" to a local Internet party, and for the first time I met THUMPER101 (aka Mike, my husband). He was there with a date (who drank too much and basically passed out). He was quite charming, and although I was 100% sure I'd never date him, I enjoyed talking to him, and he made me laugh. Somehow at the end of the evening he ended up with my number. He called, e-mailed me often, and over a short time, he quietly won over my heart. I still to this day don't know what happened. We've been together ever since (four years) and will be married three years this November.

110. *Ask for the middle seat*

Holly Grubs (an attorney who volunteers for the homeless): *I always opt for the middle seat on an airplane. I met a great guy this way. We had a distraction-free chat for the entire trip and since then have dated when we're in the same place/same time. Unfortunately our schedules and locations have not allowed much more . . . yet.*

Betsy Odita (an investment adviser): *I was heading with some friends to the JazzFestival and was late boarding, so my friends were already ensconced. I was assigned a middle seat, but sat in the window seat. A man (we'd hit it off when we conversed briefly before boarding) followed me onto the plane and came towards my row. I assumed I was in his window seat and moved to the center seat. He took the window; we conversed for the entire two-hour flight and made plans to meet up again in New Orleans.*

We've been together ever since. He moved from Chicago to New York City to be with me. We plan to be married next May.

111. *The beach*

April Martin (an ex-ballerina, flamenco dancer, a shoe/clotheshorse "with a third degree black belt in shopping," April is a program manager at Sun Microsystems): *Hit the waves. The beach. It's a wonderful thing with or without men. I happen to live a five-minute bike ride away, so I'm lucky. When the sea is really brewing, I can hear her waves crashing and she lulls me to sleep.*

I've been "approached," shall we say, at the beach while sunning and reading, but I normally just politely "shoo" the ones who are trolling. What can I say? I'm a tough nut to crack, and those surfer types always seem a bit sophomoric.

However, one time I was running, at sunset. An attractive specimen came towards me on his run and smiled. I waved back (it's the polite thing to do round these parts), and within 10 minutes I could hear steps padding, plodding, and thudding behind me.

I whipped my head around to make sure the plodder behind me didn't have a blunt object and saw that it was, in fact, smiley-pants. I kept running until I had no more beach left (!!) to run on and had to turn around. As I did, he smiled again and said, "Aren't you ever going to stop running so I can ask you out?"

The poor thing was knackered and looked as if he might drop! But I had to decline. You see, I've been spoken for (no, not married) and am one of those faithful types. He was darling and I just might have taken him up on his offer if . . .

There's so much more, but I have a slab of fresh tuna waiting for me to sear it.

112. *Know how to handle your stick*

Stephanie McDonald (a medical-office manager who's currently applying for Baylor College of Medicine's egg-donor program because she'd "like to help an infertile couple achieve their dream"): *In my personal experience, pool halls are the best place—and the high-testosterone guys who inhabit these places are always impressed with a woman who can handle her stick.*

(NOTE: You may now bid melodious adieu to the pool hall idea.)

113. *Go for the shy ones at parties*

Christie Haney (a single mother and a Ph.D. candidate in international peace and conflict resolution, Christie works construction during the summer and rock climbs):

One of the best ways to meet men is to single out the ones who hang near the outskirts of a party or club. They are the shy ones, instead of the really boisterous ones I usually go for. The quiet fellows are just as cute, but are not the "players" I end up falling for and then hating.

114. *Take up motorcycling*

Lou Iannone (is from British Columbia and works with the Interior Health Authority): *Last weekend my friend and I had to halt at a rest stop to use the ladies' room. When I came out, my friend was talking to a very good-looking man who also happened to be riding a motorcycle. He also happened to turn out to be a doctor. He called her the next day. They have a date scheduled this very evening.*

115. *Weddings*

April Morris (art consultant): *Just met the man o' my dreams at a close friend's wedding. We were both in the wedding party. And during the reception we were enraptured with one another. All dressed up and strolling through the city park late at night—bliss, sheer bliss. Yes, weddings it is! Wish me luck! He's scrumptious!*

Thank you, my friends!

The One-Mile Limit

Statistics predict you'll marry a man who lives within a mile of your house, so . . .

116. *Eat your lunch at the same time on the same park bench near your office every day. (That way the God of Statistics knows where to find you.)*

117. *Nature hikes/bird-watching near your home. The writer Sue Halpern, in an op-ed piece in* The New York Times, *quotes Camilla Blackman: "People go all over the world to see giraffes, but take them into their backyards and they don't know what they're seeing." Exactly.*

118. *Your town meetings about environmental "issues." These are weirder than you can ever imagine. Earnest men shouting about the new Wal-Mart taking away vital swampland. Such passion! Such shouting! Such drama! Great place to meet guys!*

119. *Any street fair, farmers' market, pumpkin festival, etc., near your abode.*

Uh. About that "mile from your house" statistic. I don't have the foggiest idea where it originates. I've seen it printed in several books. Nobody gives the source. I detest and loathe them all! It seems to me three miles would be more in the zone of probability. That's the range, according to AAA, in which most accidents occur.

Okay. Doll, let's wrap it up. This is not the time to stay in the house watching *Friends* reruns. Not the time to rigidly adhere to the same strategy day after day. One bold stroke and you win! And if you lose a few times, so what? There are *hundreds* of fine opportunities for you to run amok with. Did I say hundreds? Pooh, 6,244,938,437 people live on this planet, which means roughly 3.5 billion men exist. Of those 3.5 billion men, 850 million will be in your age range. Of those 850 million in your age range, about 70 million will possess many of the high-grade Olympian-ish attributes you're looking for in a man—*70 million!*

The secret is to place yourself where the highest numbers of those 70 million live right here in the old U.S. of A. Which is what the last 50 pages of this book have been about. (Also, because Ma Nature is choosy about finding her novel gene combinations, the more men you meet, the higher your chances Ma will select the perfect chap for you to click with.) Or, hell, junk the whole thing and follow your gut. Because here's what, Kumquat:

With the right attitude (Week One), the right look (Week Two), a little bit of grit (Week Three), huge numbers of eligible chaps (Week Four), meeting your dream man becomes *inescapable.* And what happens next?

DEAR E. JEAN: I'm 25, funny, sophisticated, and appealing. But for some reason, whenever I meet a guy I'm interested in, I end up stammering nervously and making a complete fool of myself. Of course when a guy I'm NOT attracted to comes on to me, I have NO butterflies. The flirtatious remarks fly out of my mouth. Help!

—Totally Mystified

YOU TWITTERING FRET-WAFFLE: You're SUPPOSED to be nervous, Miss Totally. Butterflies are the sign—didn't you see the Disney classic, for Gawdsake?—your Snow White Moment may be about to happen . . .

Week Five:
You See Him . . . and You
Absolutely Lose Your Brain

Or

You Meet and You Sorta Like Him

OK. So.

You're heading toward Rocco's Shoe Repair shop and you've got your squirrel-chasing-garbage-eating-crotch-sniffing dog on a leash and your cowgirl boots under your arm, and now it starts to rain. Your hair, which was a frizz ball when you left, is now exploding in all directions, looking like three pounds of packing peanuts are growing from your scalp. And because you're glancing at your reflection in the shop windows and wishing to heaven you could send your hair back to your apartment to be ironed, you nearly run over a baby in a stroller. When you reach Rocco's Repair place, SWOOSH! JINGLE JINGLE! the door opens, a man comes out—a man ineffably delicious, a man of exactly the right height, a man

with dark eyes, and he pauses to hold the door for you . . . and because you *know that falling in love is your major errand in life* . . .
and because you don't lack heart . . . and because you're ready to
seize that trollop Fate by her topaz belly ring and because . . .

Your Brain Is an Expertly Curated Museum, It Recognizes a Masterpiece When It Sees Him

. . . and since it only takes a fraction of a second for *him* to recog-
nize you as his Dazzling Princess Charming, then, by God, the next
thing you must do is . . .

?

Let's review. You remember the Snow White Effect? You remember Dr. Frank Bernieri and his bleeding-edge research,
which shows that when two people meet and "click," their bodies
flow into synchrony, and it's so indescribably delightful it looks
like a *dance*? And you remember the Snow White Effect happens
in the first 30 seconds, or it pretty much doesn't happen *ever*? You
recall this, don't you, Doll? And since you possess an IQ of blinding altitude, you also remember the old gals, your foremothers,
may not have been a wholesome lot, but they knew about males
and sex and the power to enthrall because every single one of
your foremoms aroused every single one of your foredads, or you
would not be here reading this annoying "you remember" para-
graph?

Right?

So, now all you have to do is:

Man Catching Law #5
Get Out of Your Own Way.

The whole thing is being handed to you. So . . . as you stand there in the doorway of Rocco's with your cowgirl boots and your crotch-sniffing dog, glance up at the dark-eyed fellow and *at least not TRY to pull off an act.*

Because, believe me, Honey, you're *already* in the midst of giving a Hepburn-grade performance:

1. *You've launched into a natural sequence of head-tilting, eyebrow-lifting, pupil-dilating, and eyeball-glistening.*

2. *In a blinding flash you're taking in the man's shoulders, hair, eyes, teeth, chin, jaws, beard stubble, pallor/ruddiness, symmetry of features, height, biceps, shoulder-waist ratio, hips and doodlebanger; you're evaluating his age, sexual prowess, and health.*

2a. *His wardrobe is giving you his income, background, parentage, probable occupation, emotional maturation, and God knows what other galvanic personal turn-ons— his banana-cream-colored shirt is setting off the blinding (well, why do I keep saying blinding? You're seeing as clearly as you've ever seen in your life at this moment), setting off a sudden, prescient intuition that you can not go on living without the man in Rocco's doorway.*

3. *As quickly as your pupils dilate, you down-lash and look away. This is innate.*

4. *Your lips grow redder, redder, redder, redder . . . you burst into a smile.*

Note: Dr. Monica Moore, a psychologist from Webster University in St. Louis, observed women's "attraction maneuvers" at parties, restaurants, and bars for two thousand hours. (My dear Dr. Moore, that's a lot of chardonnay spritzers!)

And what did the doctor discover? That women send "initial" signals to men two-thirds of the time—i.e., flirt first. And here's the fascinating part: The women who enticed the most chaps were not the prettiest, but the ones who sent the most signals.

5. *You angle your head down and sideways—and here comes the man-killer—you glance up again, through your lashes. (A flagwoman signaling a 747 on the runway for takeoff is nothing to YOU, darling.)*

6. *You are picking up his scent. You're reading each other's racy passages in your DNA diaries.*

Note: #6 is just a hunch of mine. But Dr. Martha McClintock of the University of Chicago has found hard evidence that you're a sucker for a man who smells like you do, but not exactly like you do; and that you're catalyzed into a near lust-craze by a man who smells like your dad—but, again, not precisely like your dad.

Dr. McClintock's theory is you're searching for an immune system that is compatible with your own, but different enough to provide your offspring with protection against infection.

Hence, my friend Marsha Pinkstaff (you recall Marsha and the Kentucky Derby Man-Staring Adventure) came home from a first date the other night with a tall, handsome, rich, M&A guy with a house in the Hamptons,

$600,000 *a year, and a twelve-room apartment on 71st and Madison; and left the following message on my machine:*

"Uuulllk! I didn't like his smell!"

6a. *Charles Wysocki, adjunct professor at the University of Pennsylvania, writing in the* Journal of Biology of Reproduction, *has discovered that "male perspiration had a beneficial effect on women's moods." His study suggests that male sweat helps women feel less tense and raises reproductive-hormone levels. Researchers collected samples from the undeodorized armpits of male volunteers, mixed them into a cocktail, and applied it to the upper lips of 18 women. Will these researchers stop at nothing? Lawzy!*

7. *Meanwhile, the air running through his voice box at 500 cycles per second is notifying you (your unconscious is quite the little Hilton sister) of his position in society.*

NOTE: Yes, things have come to such a pass that psychologists are now studying the air in your windpipe. Drs. Stanford W. Gregory Jr. and Timothy J. Gallagher of Kent State University discovered this little microbrew of social-rank-revealing wind. John Schwartz of The New York Times, *reporting on the phenomenon, compared it to the "hum of bagpipes." So if the guy in the doorway occupies a social sphere above you, you will alter your bagpipe hum to match his. If you are above him, he will adapt his.*

8. *And if that isn't enough, your poor brain, which just a second before couldn't give two aesthetic shits who was in the damn shoe-repair shop, is now busy soaking itself*

*down in a phenylethylamine bath of lust and exhilara-
tion (this may actually be the chemical that causes
"clicking"—it speeds up the gush of information between nerve cells, which is why falling in love "at first
sight" is so euphoric), your stress levels (heartbeat, blood
pressure) are rising . . .*

9. *The fabulous Dr. Helen Fisher is putting lovers through
MRI brain-scanners (probably as you read this) to prove
levels of dopamine and norepinephrine elevate when you
see someone you love.*

   *Plus Dr. Fisher believes "naturally occurring am-
phetamines pool in the emotional centers of the brain"
and that's why lovers feel they are "speeding."*

10. *So thank God you've got the dog. The little cur is as good
as a Xanax.*

   *NOTE: People in the company of their dog or cat
dealt better with stress than people who were alone or
accompanied by a friend or spouse in research con-
ducted by Dr. Karen Allen of the State University of New
York.*

And may I just say this whole doorway scene with the "undeodorized armpits," etc., etc., is becoming quite stressful to old
yours truly—with the phenylethylamine baths, etc., etc., and the
bagpipes, etc., etc.,—which is why I am now going to turn things
over to beautiful Dr. Nalini Ambady, head of the Interpersonal Per-
ception and Communication Laboratory at Harvard. [Ambady and
Frank Bernieri, close friends, are the Watson and Crick of "thin
slices"—spontaneous social judgments we make from very brief
(less than five seconds) observations of behavior.]

E: Doctor, how can a woman make a dazzling first impression on a member of the opposite sex?

Dr. Ambady: It depends on what the member of the opposite sex is looking for. Is he looking for someone who is extroverted, kind of peppy with lots of energy? Or is he looking for someone who is more thoughtful and reserved? But, of course, she wouldn't know if she's never met him. So I'd say, be true to yourself. When you fake it, people see through it really fast, because you're uncomfortable, right?

E: I've had some long talks with Dr. Frank Bernieri.

Dr. Ambady: He's a very good friend.

E: He seems to believe that if you don't hit it off pretty quickly in the beginning, it's extremely difficult to correct that. Do you agree?

Dr. Ambady: *At that time,* yes. But on subsequent interactions, I believe it *is* possible. We can all think of people we misjudged and we got to like them a lot later.

E: Ok. This is good news. So let's say we make a terrific first impression. Kaboom! The hearts are racing, the eyes are twinkling, pizzazzy chemicals are coursing through our brains. How can we maintain that lovely feeling for the second, third, fourth times we see each other?

Dr. Ambady: If you have that initial very good rapport, chances are excellent that it can be re-created. It will follow. It can be reestablished.

E: How do we do that?

Dr. Ambady: There's no "how to." These behaviors work best when they are nonconscious. It *can't* be created *intentionally.* So that makes it really hard to answer the "how to" questions. Because you *can't*.

E: So you're saying if we're just ourselves—

Dr. Ambady: Yes. Be natural! Because what happens if you plan too much and you're very strategic and you're worried about, I don't know, how your hands are placed, or whether you're having good eye contact or not, then you're *worried* about *that* and you're not paying attention to the person.

E: Exactamo!

Dr. Ambady: And *that's* what is going to come through. So letting you're natural instincts guide you is important. If we overthink things, there's a lot of evidence that we fall on our faces. [*NOTE: Dr. Ambady is leading the field in studying this "fall on your face if you overreflect" phenomenon.*] We've found that if people overthink, they tend to make worse decisions than if they just go with their instincts. Those are better.

E: Do you know how many romance self-help books are out there telling women how to "think"?

(Dr. Ambady chuckles. We are on the phone. Her voice is soft and melodious and her chuckle is like crinkling back the cellophane wrapper from a stick of licorice.)

Dr. Ambady: If you're manipulative—if you start a relationship being manipulative, it doesn't forebode a happy ending.

E: And the poor schmo you're manipulating falls for the phony you're *playing* so . . .

Dr. Ambady: You have to keep up the charade.

(Excited pause.)

E: Can we adore someone at first sight?

Dr. Ambady: Yes. You can be *very* attracted to people at first sight.

E: But how is it possible? Can you explain it to me?

Dr. Ambady: Getting back to Frank's work, it's probably a matter of rapport or a spark or simply a *match.*

E: Why are we so worried, then?

Dr. Ambady: Because we know that first impressions count. The best thing is to just enjoy who you are, enjoy the moment you're in, and feel that things will take care of themselves. *[Surprised at herself]* I sound like a—

E: You sound like a brilliant woman, Doctor. Thank you!

Ok. Now. There you are in the rainy entrance of Rocco's Shoe Repair shop with your hair twice the size it was before reading the Nalini Ambady interview. Your eyes—is there something wrong with your eyes?—your pupils have expanded to the size of Florentine olives. Your cheeks are as flushed as a five-year-old's after playing with her mother's rouge. Your dog is going at the pants of the handsome banana-cream-shirted stranger as if there's a sirloin stapled in his boxers. What now?

Well, now you will hold the chap there for 30 seconds.

Why?

Because your affair with this man will inspire the world to greatness . . . and for synchrony to occur—and synchrony is what starts everything boiling furiously, or, excuse me, synchrony is the result of everything (love/lust/intrigue/interest) beginning to boil furiously—you need to be body-to-body, cherry-red-smile-to-cherry-red-smile, DNA-to-DNA, for several moments. I don't need to explain why you absolutely must synchronize, do I, Doll?

Because when you *syn* (from the Greek meaning "coming together"), you'll prolong the *chron,* i.e., the time. And when you're *synching* and *chroning,* you'll both feel the rush-rush and the gush-gush of happiness, and then chances are excellent neither of you will be able to resist the impulse of exchanging phone numbers.

But he is coming *out* of Rocco's. You are going in. This is not going to be easy. It'd be a snap if you were standing in the Hertz line at the Detroit airport, or loading up your enchiladas in the commissary at NBC . . . *anywhere* but in this wet doorway. And how do you stop him? Well, Doll, you have to say something. Yes. You must make a remark. You must grab this moment, grasp it at its zenith, and its zenith is *now.* Even if you're not good at moment-grasping, even if you've never thought of yourself as a grasper of moments, you must grasp this one, open your mouth and speak.

"Emph!" you say—the last thing you need to do at this point is send your brain, which is already *soaking* with weird sex chemicals, careening around your skull like a Ping-Pong ball to try to come up with a "witty" remark—so, you say:

"Emph! This rain!"

"Really coming down," he says, and keeps walking out the door.

![1]

---

1. Shiiiiiiiiiit!

Let's back up. You are going *into* the shoe repair shop. He is coming *out*. Oh, look. He's holding the door for you. Now for godsakes, THIS time if you're completely paralyzed, if you have the brain of a newborn, an imbecile, a flea, if you become suddenly aphasic, please refer, for strength and sustenance, to The All-Time Queenhell Showstoppers:

I. The Shirt Salutation

This is just ridiculously successful.

A. *You see him.*

B. *You like him.*

C. *You say, "Lawsamercy! Love your shirt!"*

D. *You don't have to say* lawsamercy; *but you* honestly *must like the shirt.*

E. *He'll be charmed. He'll be enchanted. He'll say something like "I've got a man in England who buys my shirts. He sends over a selection at the beginning of each season, spring and fall."*

F. *You will now do one of two things:*

> **1.** The *Great Gatsby:* Bend your head into his chest like Daisy Buchanan and begin to cry stormily. "This is such a beautiful shirt. It makes me sad because I've never seen such—such a beautiful shirt before."

> **2.** The *Mr. Right, Right Now!:* With a bewitching murmur, you will say you wish to buy one exactly like it for your brother/father/boss—and where did he purchase it.

G. Enthralling conversation ensues.

H. Also works with shoes and watches.

II. Drop Him a Curtsy

This little maneuver is so unexpected, so surprising, so new, so old, so amusing, so charming, so Michelle-Pfeiffer-*Dangerous-Liaisons*-delicious, you can't *get* any more appealing. I *am* serious. If you can be yourself and manage it—i.e., if you possess a drop of the dramatic—you can pull it off. Now don't sit there, Doll Face, and tell me you don't know *how* to bob a damn curtsy . . .

A. You smile.

B. You incline your head.

C. You bat lash.

D. You place your right leg slightly behind your left, with the tip of your right toe placed about four inches to the left of your left heel.

E. You sweep your arms out prettily to either side about the width of a farthingale.

F. You bend your left knee four inches—and dip.

G. Your eyes flutter up to his face as you rise.

H. The whole thing—lash bat, arm-sweep, bob—takes maybe a second and a half.

I. *The man will stand in front of you, his mouth hanging open like a ham, absolutely* staggered. *He will feel that something strange, something extraordinary, something* magic, *has just occurred.*

J. *The author wishes to acknowledge she is a very big fan of this one; but it is showy and not many women can follow the main premise of* Mr. Right, Right Now!*—be yourself—and fricking curtsy.*

III. Hem and Haw like Annie Hall

Stammering, blushing, repeating yourself, forgetting what you were about to say, swallowing, snorting, gagging, coughing, yelping, giggling—all are enchanting in a Drew-Barrymore-*Never-Been-Kissed,* Sandra-Bullock-*While-You-Were-Sleeping* kind of way. The truth is, as many men are inflamed by lack-of-confidence women as are inflamed by your chock-full types. So don't fret if you're not pulling off an extremely happening hello—just stand there and stammer.

IV. The Hair Hi

Men are weak and flighty when it comes to their hair. If they are susceptible to the beguilements of Hair Clubs, what might not the breezy Hair Hi do to their fragile psyches? So . . .

A. *You see a man you've never seen before.*

B. *You raise your eyes to his hair and almost gasp at its virility, its beauty; and then stepping slightly backward:*

You: I like your haircut!

Him (surprised): Thanks!

You: Who cuts it? I'd like to tell my brother/boss/father.

Him (realizing at last he's found the woman who will provide the stability, the joy, the serenity, the purity of life, he's always searched for): May I take your clothes off immediately?

Of course you'll make these little "stoppers" your own. You'll bend them and twist them; but you won't believe how incredibly *well* they work when you're loading a hot dog with relish at the Blackhawks game, or strolling into the Executive Dining Room, or buying *Don Giovanni* at Tower Records, or standing in the wings wearing a pair of unprecedentedly high heels waiting to give the keynote speech at the Nature Conservancy fund-raiser, or walking into Rocco's repair shop on a rainy Saturday with your dog and you're both shaking the water drops from your hair and you stop . . . and you say to the dark-eyed man holding the door for you:

"Hey, uh, I like, you know . . . *nice* shirt. Where'd you get it?"

And the man smiles.

And you smile.

And he smiles.

"Honey," he says, raising his voice slightly, "where'd we get this shirt?"

And the woman with the baby in the stroller on the sidewalk behind you, says:

"I think we got it at Banana Republic."

· · · ·

And all that dramatic dopamine that has burst loose and has been running riot, overflowing your neural banks, begins to recede, your pupils dwindle to tiny specks, a fitz of regret rolls around your spinal column, and Ok. At least you did it. You got in some *practice*. "Certainly not a wasted effort," you're saying to yourself as you walk into the shop, glance through your hair (which is now the size of Iowa), and are suddenly dragged *over* the counter and into the shoe shelf by your comical, mud-flecked cur, who has just spotted the cobbler's cat.

You drop your boots on the counter.

"Ah, she love my Caesar!" says Rocco, the shop owner, laughing pleasantly and handing you (you've been through this before with Rocco) the pickup receipt. You retrieve the panting hound. She is scowling at you with an expression that says, "The very first meaningful relationship I've come across all day and *you* spoil everything," and out the door you hurry, scolding, "You incorrigible strumpet"—and down the street—"you insolent baggage"—the dog adores this kind of talk—"you jilt, you saucy chops . . ."

Just as you reach the corner you hear running steps behind you . . . and turn.

"You dropped this," he says.

He is holding a wallet.

"Oh!" You're all amazement.

"I . . . I . . . I . . . I . . . ," you say.

You've rarely seen such fine exterior attractions—height, elegance, build, beat leather jacket—all the more interesting because the combination looks *fantastic* in the midst of this heavy rain.

"I . . . I . . . I . . ."

Your poor cake of a brain, which just had all its candles blown out a minute before, is suddenly refrosted, relit, put back on the platter, while the neurons that were in *no mood* are now flicking on and starting to sing.

"It's yours, isn't it?" he says, smiling.

You can barely drag your eyes away from his teeth. Dazzling! Gleaming! You glance at the thing in his hand.

It looks familiar, vaguely, you seem to remember the color, dimly, the shape is . . . well, no doubt it's your wallet, but you don't care if it's your wallet, you don't care if you ever see another wallet again as long as you live, because all is over. The gods have smote you. Smote? Lord.

What a day—huh?—when you're thinking of things like being *smote.*

But whatever your atavistic gut reaction is, whatever ancient combination of sexy foremother instincts, whatever the lessons contained in your corpuscles, whatever that combination of elements— they *all* kick in, KABOOM! You don't have to do a damn thing. Just let it happen. And your face lights up with a nectared radiance, and—

"Thanks!" you say.

"That's all right," he says.

"Really!"

"Yeah."

"Thank you!"

"You're welcome."

(Laughter.)

"It's incredible."

"What?"

"Oh—" You shake your head.

"What . . . ?" he says.

"Nothing."

"What?"

(Laughter.)

"Nothing."

"What?"

"I—can't . . ." You shake your head again.

"What?"

(Laughter.)

"No."

(Laughter.)

"What?"

(Laughter.)

This is flirting.

All you need is a pair of eyes, a tight sweater, a tube of spankin'-red lipstick, and you'll squash the hearts and mangle the brains of three-quarters of the men on the sidewalk. Hell, you don't even need the sweater or the lipstick. The Corpus Juris of Flirting can be contained in . . .

Man Catching Law #6
Torture Your Victim.

Vex him! Thrash him! Keep him off-balance! Even if you possess not a cc of CC (coquetry courage), throw a mischievous smile in his direction while you're saying "Thank you," then drop your eyes. (This will come naturally to you; just don't squash it. It's what lionesses, tigresses, and nanny goatesses do. It's one of the opening moves of your inborn courtship pattern.) While he's saying "You're welcome," tilt your head away and gaze back at him through your lashes. When his eyes meet yours, look away and laugh. A moment later, open your eyes wide and gaze straight at him. By this time the poor fellow (who never knew or cared to know you were on the planet and who was only doing a good deed by returning your wallet) will be rather excited.[2]

A protracted afternoon of this torment and the man will be filled with such unbearable longing for your next glance, he'll try to give you *his* wallet.

Why?

Man Catching Law #7
The Goal of Flirting Is Love.
(All right, all right, the goal of flirting is also sex.)

&

Man Catching Law #8
The Essence of Romantic Love (and Sex) Is Uncertainty.

Uncertainty will be created if, when you converse with the chap, you show not the slightest concern whether he lives or drops dead—while at the same time entrancing him with your fire-apple-red lips and saucy flicks of real admiration, as in "My dog likes people; but I've *never* seen her tear the zipper off anyone's jeans!"

---

2. This is just the old *inborn* look/look-away courting behavior. Formal name: The Coy Look. It entices just as well with some *distance*—e.g., across a crowded law library, executive sales conference, hotel gym, Bergdorf's Men's Store, Sing Sing's visitors' waiting room.

Questions? Yes, you.

You: When you say "you," as in "when you converse with the chap," who do you mean? Who's *you*?

Eeee: I mean you. You, the incredibly charming reader of *Mr. Right, Right Now!*

You: I thought so. Cool! Ok. So, I've kept him there for 30 seconds. Now what?

Eeee: Well . . . are you clicking?

You: I think so.

Eeee: Then don't stop.

You: Don't stop what?

Eeee: Don't stop what you're doing.

You: What am I doing?

Eeee: You're doing plenty, believe me.

You: But what should I *do*?

Eeee: Tell him what you're doing next.

You: What am I doing next?

Eeee: Getting some coconut cream pie.

You: Pie? I tell him I'm getting some coconut cream pie? Should I invite him along?

Eeee: No. Just state the fact: "I'm on my way to get some coconut cream pie."

You: Then he'll say *he* wants pie too?

Eeee: Exactly. You turn it into an occasion.

You: You mean a first date!

Eeee: No such thing as "first dates."

You: Whew.

Eeee: Just clicking and synchronizing.

You: What if he doesn't like me?

Eeee: Would you *stop*? You're going for coconut cream pie. No big deal. If you expect nothing, if you want nothing, you'll be *full* of power.

You (apprehensively): Ok.

Eeee: Ok?

You: . . . Ok.

Eeee: Don't think. Forget yourself. Think of pie.

You: Coconut cream pie?

Eeee: Correct.

You: One thing.

Eeee: What?

You: How do I know he's Mr. Right?

Eeee: You don't.

You: Humph! How can you go around calling this book *Mr. Right, Right Now!* and—

Eeee: Because Ma Nature's *telling* you he's Mr. Right and she's telling you he's standing in front of your eyes *right now.*

You: Ok, so he *is* Mr. Right.

Eeee: Shhhush! The moment you start thinking he's Mr. Right— *that's* the DEATH MOMENT. You may as well give up men and start ordering the $279 dolls from Marie Osmond on the Home Shopping Network. Because when you begin believing he's Mr. Right—just a minute. This is a big deal. I better make this a law:

Man Catching Law #9
Never Decide He's "The One."

You: Never? Why not?

Eeee: Because the moment you *decide* he's The One, the moment you make-up your mind and tell yourself that he *is,* indeed, Mr. Right, that's the moment you totally lose it and start focusing all your desires on him . . . and when you focus all your desires on him, you become kind of paralyzed. And when you're paralyzed, you dribble away the flirtatious mystery that attracted him to you in the first place. And when you lose your attraction, he starts to turn off. And when he starts to turn off, you act with less confidence. And when you act with less confidence, he pulls away. And when he pulls away, you go crazy because you think he's Mr. Right, and you start to cling. And when you cling, he leaves. So stop thinking about it.

You: But shouldn't I have a checklist? I mean, shouldn't I check if he has at least *some* of the qualities I want in my Mr. Right?

Eeee: Well . . . how many qualities are on your list?

You: I'm excessively picky, you know. I have at least 40 things I'm looking for.

Eeee: Phooo! Mother Nature has 44 *thousand* items on her list—maybe more —and Ma's checking every single gene on every one of his 46 chromosomes. She's checking his IQ, his life expectancy, his sperm count, his allergy to marshmallows, his cholesterol, how far he can throw a football, his love of children, and his tendency to adore women with small breasts. The old dame wants her smart, strong, sexy new gene-combinations and she's obviously *nuts* about this guy.

You: Why do you say *obviously*?

Eeee: 'Cause you're acting giddier than Carmen Electra in a tattoo parlor.

You: Yeah [giggling], I feel like I'm flying.

Eeee: That's Ma firing your dopamine circuits.

You: What about *his* circuits?

Eeee: *Your* circuits are playing off *his* circuits. The more rapidly his dopamine system fires, the more rapidly yours will fire. And vice versa. A neuroscientist, Dr. P. Read Montague, calls this "entraining."

You: But . . . but . . .

Eeee: Now what?

You: I don't have a dog. What's with this stupid dog you've given me?

Eeee: An event on the level of birth or death is happening and you are complaining about a *dog*?

You: Well . . .

Eeee: Her name is Fortuna de la Spunky. You rescued her last winter. She's the best dog in the world. Are you going to be an anecdote in this book, or not?

You: Ok. Ok. Ok, don't get hissy.

So, you say:

"Gee, I was going to go to Pet's Mart to get *this totally brilliant dog* a new Frisbee, but this rain puts me in mind of banana cream pie."

And he says, because he's not certain (and the essence of love is uncertainty) if this is an invitation:

"Banana cream pie! Man, I *love* banana cream pie. I even love banana cream pie when the bananas turn all brown. I'll eat the whole pie when it's banana cream pie. Everything about banana cream pie, Jesus, just mention banana cream pie and I'm a goner."

Now you say:

"*Oop!* I didn't mean banana cream pie, I meant coconut cream pie."

"Coconut cream pie!" he says. "Even better. If God ate pie, She'd eat coconut cream pie."

"I wonder where somebody could *find* coconut cream pie?" Again. Not an invitation.

And he says: "Betty's Café over on Twelfth Street. You want to walk over?"

And you say: "Sure."

And he says: "If you don't mind going out of the way two blocks, we could pick up *my* dog, Charlie."

And you say: "What fun!" Because you've just followed . . .

Man Catching Law #10
Turn the First Encounter into an Event.

You: And now what?

Eeee: Pie.

You: But how do I act?

Eeee: *No* acting.

You: Could you get off your ass and help me here? What am I supposed *do.*

Eeee: You've done it. You met someone. You completed the Supreme
Moment. The old world is destroyed. The new world is now.
Everything from this moment on is fresh, green, new, cool.

And here you are outside Betty's Café, at a table on the sidewalk, in
the rain, eating pie. The dogs are also eating pie. Your cell phone
rings.

"Hi, Dad!" you say, laughing. . . . "Oh, nothing. Having a bite.
How's Mom?"

"Let me talk to him," says the guy, putting down his fork and
smiling.

"At Betty's Café," you say.

"Let me speak with him," says the fellow, wiping his lips with a
blue Betty's napkin.

He is so good-humored and handsome, even the pigeons on the
street seem delighted with him.

"No, over on Twelfth Street," you say.

"May I speak with him?" says the fellow.

"Dad, there's someone here who wants to talk with you," you say, laughing.

You hand him the phone.

"Hello, Mr. Smith," says the guy. "How do you do, sir? I admire your daughter more than I can say. She's everything I've been looking for and I would like to ask you, sir, for her hand in marriage."

DEAR E. JEAN: How do I ask a man out? Now that I know I must go out and **FIND** a man, I realize I may even have to do the asking. But how do I go about it? It's a complete mystery to me. I've spent the better part of my 29 years learning to be "a lady" and waiting for **MEN** to ask **ME**. HELP!! —Needing Beta-Blockers

BLOCKERS, YOU BEAUTY: First, let's set the record straight: IF my mother had not asked my father to her sorority ski weekend in the Sierra Nevada, I would not be here writing about asking a man . . .

Week Five 1/2:
How to Ask a Man Out

Before we commence, let's get the phone stuff out of the way:

> *Man Catching Law #11*
> *Handing a Man Your Number Is Dumb.*
> *Why Don't You Just Go Down on Your*
> *Knees on the Sidewalk and <u>Beg</u>*
> *the Bugger to Call You?*

When you meet a man in person (not on-line), if there are any numbers given out, you will *exchange* them, and not a numeral less. (That way you can call him, if he doesn't call you.[1]) And when you write the numbers down, don't be stingy. Take up space. Write on something unforgettable:

---

1. Oh, pick yourself up off the linoleum, Doll. Yes, you can call him. As many men are lathered up by being called by a charming woman as are *not* lathered.

1. *The windshield of his car in topaz eye shadow.*

2. *Trees. All kinds of lovey-dovey can blossom in the 19 or 20 hours it takes to whittle the suckers into the bark of an oak.*

3. *His biceps. And if you don't make a fuss over your "8s and 6s" growing "bigger than cantaloupes" when he flexes his muscles, you don't deserve to fulfill your destiny. Meanwhile ask him to write his number on the bill of your Seahawks cap—it will become a talisman for your courtship. Every time you wear it, he'll remember bells ringing in his head and how the pen shook in his hand with excitement as he wrote.*

4. *Your sock. Take off your boot and Sharpie your number on your pink argyle and hand it to him. And ask him do the same—if he refuses to write on his sock, make him remove his T-shirt.*

5. *A $10 bill. Jot your number on one half, ask him to write his on the other half, tear it in two—it's even more memorable if it's a $50 bill.*

6. *All this is sounding very Ladies' Magazine to me.*

7. *If you're hot stuff in the confidence department, do the opposite—write on something fleeting and mercurial: form the numbers with seaweed, sand, etc., etc., if you're at the beach (on the wind and stars if you're elsewhere), and the chap will gallop all over hell and back looking for something "permanent" to write with/on like a hot-dog-bun wrapper and a piece of charcoal.*

8. *I always liked Ladies' Magazines.*

9. *I'm avoiding the obvious here—punching the numbers into your cell phone—because I've received just one too many letters where numbers have been lost.[2] Go ahead and do it. But make certain the digits are saved.*

And then . . .

Man Catching Law #12
Do Not Care If He Calls.

In fact . . .

---

2. *DEAR E. JEAN: HELP! EMERGENCY! TRAGEDY! Last night I met the handsomest, most charming Irish fellow. It was one of those chance encounters people talk about. When I least expected it, I met the man of my dreams. I was so smitten, I actually asked for his number. (Something I've never done before.) He gave it to me on the condition I PROMISE to call him. I punched it into my cell phone before I left the bar. Today I discovered his number's not been saved!*

I can't accept that I'll never see him again! I've had a long run of bad luck trying to meet a "quality" man. It's unbearable living on the hope we'll happen to catch the same subway train or pass each other on the street. He said he lives only ten minutes from me. What should I do? He was right in front of my eyes, and now he's out of reach!—Desperately Seeking in Brooklyn

I told Miss Desp. that assuming she'd downed a half-pint of Finnian's Red (to honor the fates) and tried calling the bar to interview the bartender, I believed I could absolutely guarantee that if she returned to the saloon where they first met, she'd see the lad again, because being Irish myself, I could confirm that an Irishman is as loyal to his favorite pub as Bono is to his blue glasses, and that NEXT time, for Godsakes, write the phone numbers on something MEMORABLE.

Man Catching Law #13
Do Not EXPECT Him to Call.

Indeed . . .

Man Catching Law #14
You Will Lower Your Frustration Level
If You Never Expect Men to Do ANYTHING.

The reason we become so angry at men (and exasperated with "dating" and peeved at "love") is that we possess perilously optimistic ideas about what men and "romance" are like. Really now, we'll only stop being pissed off when we stop hoping (and what an evil, suckery thing *hope* is) men will turn out to be perfect.

One more thing.

If you're going to call him, call him at a time when you're pretty certain he won't be tired or with a patient or watching a game or entertaining a girl named Twirly. Sometimes it's wise to send him an e-mail with a couple of charming lines and a "call me" and your number. *Then* if he doesn't call, you call him.

How to Ask a Man Out

Forget the total bushwa about not asking men out.

If those two charming dingbats[3] who wrote *The Rules* (i.e., "Don't talk to a man first, don't ask him to dance," don't open your

---

3. I'm sorry to harp on these two deluded old ladies, but they mangled many women's brains, and wrecked years of havoc, fakery, and unhappiness upon the human race by telling women to shut up and act dumb.

mouth, don't move, don't breathe, don't blink, don't live) had bothered to talk to any anthropologists, zoologists, primatologists, evolutionary biologists, or psychologists, they'd know females do as much pursuing (and "asking") as males. Indeed, chasing a man is such a successful tactic, the world is overpopulated. Hell, I may propose to the U.N. they start distributing copies of *The Rules* to employ as birth control.

Anyway, Doll, you already *know* how to ask a chap out. When you were a little girl of four, you'd pirouette up to Great-Uncle Bob and exclaim in the most confident, adorable tone, "Take me to the Dairy Queen!" And you *knew* he would do it. No man could say no to you. Because you simply *demanded* it.

So speak to men with the confidence you had at four. Practice a little by asking men any damn thing. (My mother asked my father his opinion of skiing. Soon she had whisked the dazed chap up to the High Sierra where he was forced to spend the night in a hostel with her former boyfriends, freezing his kneecaps off because he was too "gentlemanly" to knock on my mother's door and ask for a blanket. The next day on the drive back to UCLA, they fell in love at a roadside avocado stand. I was born shortly afterward with an insatiable yearning for guacamole.)

A couple days of practice will demonstrate to you that men find being asked questions *very* stimulating; and then next time you see the guy you like, grab his arm and, instead of "hello," exclaim, "Mike, you handsome rascal, I've got tickets to Usher. Let's go!"

Or,
If You INSIST
on Calling
and Asking Him Out . . .

When he answers, get right to the point:

"Michael, darling! Poker night. Next Thursday. My house. Do come!"

Or . . .

"Michael, hi. This is Eleanor Dashwood. Next Wednesday night I'm having a dinner party. Please bring your handsome self."

(Lord! These examples suck. You'll do it ten times better.)

Or, if you want to *guarantee* he'll say yes . . .

"Michael, are you sitting down? Swear you're sitting down. No. *Testify*—put your hand on your testicles—and swear you're sitting down. Good. I have ringside seats for the Lennox Lewis fight. Wanna go?"

NOTE: No "assignments" these last two weeks except the assignment where you find and seduce a mate, produce the next generation, and guarantee life's neverending blossoming and unfolding and marching onward to the everlasting glory of the earth, the galaxy, the universe, and all the billions of universes beyond.

DEAR E. JEAN: I've been noticing recently that many of my male friends have been marrying stupid women. The girls are pretty, but dull, dull, dull—so lacking in spunk and originality! I guess my real anxiety is: Will I ever find a guy to love the traits I possess—independence, creativity, humor? I'm pretty darn cute & successful as well.

—Power Girl

POWER, MY GIRL: Let me tell you a story about men and "dull" females. A few years ago, the writer Jay McInerney and his then wife, Helen Bransford, invited the 40 most eligible bachelors in New York and the 40 most intriguing single women to a posh affair, which Jay poetically referred to as a "Meet-the-Love-of-Your-Life party."

I was agog when I arrived (the guest list needed one bumbling clod—hence my invitation). The McInerney drawing room looked like a holding pen for Grand National Champion breeding bulls. "Ye gods!" I cried. "Testosterone-charged millionaires specially delivered for my own personal benefit!"

You know what? I like writing in this box so much
I just may do the whole chapter in this thing.

Anyway, ten minutes later I was standing by the bookcase, my mind fogged with one thought: "Is it possible no man is talking to me? Is it possible no man's even noticing me? Is it possible I'm the biggest loser in the room?" I glanced around to see whom the men were talking to.

Were they flocking to Martha Stewart, looking bright and horsey in khakis and hacking jacket? Were they making passes at the playwright Wendy Wasserstein, poised in Edith Sitwell black, holding a tiny plate of cheese blintzes? No. All 40 of the giddy bastards were buzzing around one small, chestnut-haired creature in a periwinkle frock (periwinkle!) perched like a butterfly on the McInerneys' giant, log-brown sofa.

Mort Zuckerman, the owner of the New York *Daily News*, looked like a eunuch on his knees before Cleopatra. Robert Morton (at the time executive producer of *Letterman*) was bringing her a glass of something—the whole room had suddenly been turned into the barbecue scene from *Gone With the Wind*. Hell, I myself felt a strong desire to bring the young lady a chicken leg. And the moral of this little story?

The girl was not a raving beauty, Miss Power; but she clearly possessed the same traits you do (independence, creativity, humor) or she would not have been at this party. The difference? She was smart enough to use ALL her assets—to put it crassly, including the ones at her admirers' eye level. (If Wendy Wasserstein had been wearing that low-cut periwinkle number, God knows what erotic chaos would have ensued—men muscling each other to the floor to get to her blintzes, Martha softly crying in the kitchen . . . scenes too marvelous to contemplate!)

Now, back to that debate: Do smart women intimidate (exhaust, frighten, annoy, repel) the men they want to attract? Yes, they do. And what tactics can an enlightened woman like you, Miss Power, employ to get around this? Read on . . .

Week Five 3/4: Intimidating the Poor Bastards? Good!

Let us leave the McInerney party for a moment and visit Oprah. She had a show recently about . . . well, I never found out what the topic was because a confused mass of "successful females" kept lunging out of their chairs and grasping, metaphorically speaking, the hem of Oprah's trousers and telling her how they "intimidated men," and how they "didn't want to intimidate men," but how they were so powerful and confident and beautiful and quite a lot of other things that their love lives were a hell on earth.

"We're gonna fricking *love* this show!" I said to the dogs, and turned up the volume.

One of the women, a strapping Midwestern blonde with pink cheeks like candy apples—superintelligent, super well-dressed, aqua-blue cashmere sweater, pearls—stood up in the audience, and as she started to speak, her face took on the expression of a woman who'd been tossed into a sawdust pit with wolverines, fought her way out, and crawled to the Harpo studio.

"Here's Miss Coup de Gracie," I said to the dogs. "Mark my word."

Her voice was pleasant but sounded a tad pinched, like it was strained through Barbara Walters's panty girdle. The list of reasons why she thought she intimidated men—devised after withstanding tortures previously unheard of, apparently—was the best yet: she was too smart, too good-looking, too happy with her life, too educated, too outgoing, and too successful. Also her "self-esteem" was "too high."

"E. Gads!" I said to the dogs. "This calls for a couple of pints of H-Dazs!"

It was clear to me, as I ripped back the lid of strawberry (for the curs) and pistachio (for myself), the poor lady had lost her mani-cured grip on reality.

My guess was early in her "amazing" career, she'd met a couple of nice blokes who, for whatever reason, ran from her like vampires from a garlic press. She'd explained their reaction to herself by say-ing, "I'm just too much for these guys."

And so, the next bloke she meets, she hardly says hello before she starts a mental rundown of her incredibly overpowering person-ality and the reasons she might be just too much for him, and kablam! She actually *does* become too much for him, because she's standing there assessing her self-presentation instead of listening and responding to the bloke.

It was a real overload of brass-busted idiocy.

Because anybody who's ever met a man knows if anything is a lethal attitude, the "I'm just too much for this guy" is a lethal atti-tude, as inevitably—in about one and a half seconds—the guy will grok that Miss Cashmere is so totally concerned with her own per-formance that she's not even noticing his dry wit, his big chest, his *GQ* cover-boy celery-green eyes, his etc., etc.

Now this is a very different attitude from the Man Catcher's sly "quit men, get men" attitude. *That's* a challenge to a bloke. That rouses his competitive instincts and vibrates in his very gizzard. This "I'm too much for him" hurts the bloke's feelings. It stings his ego because the bloke has the same insecurities that the blokette, Miss Cashmere, possesses. And when a bloke is stung, it completely closes down any chance of the bloke surprising/delighting Miss Cashmere. And when the bloke can't surprise/delight Miss Cashmere, then she can't respond in a captivating/enticing blokette manner—and that is death to clicking. And of course the bloke moves on, and Miss Cashmere finds yet another reason she's "just too much for guys" and adds it to her list, which is now so long, she has to crawl on TV and unbosom herself to Oprah—OPRAH!—who in addition to being the most intimidating and richest woman on earth is also just about the most adored.

The Truth

Look, men *do* like nonthreatening, soft little creatures. Who doesn't? We *all* slavered over the Periwinkle Girl at the McInerney party. But so what? Are you supposed to be a human speck the rest of your life? Play it safe forever? Just because a few nincompoop guys roll up like dishrags at the sight of you? (Actually Periwinkle Girl was a hero because she not only possessed a Mistress of the Universe career as a consultant, she understood the finer points of real estate by placing herself in the exact center of the room under the most flattering light.)

But Miss Cashmere? The poor lady was fading into the shadows so badly her problem was not that she was intimidating men, but that she was not intimidating men *enough*. A little fear in a chap is a good thing. Fear (F) rides in the same pair of wing tips as awe. Awe (A) leads to Love (L). Or to state the Man Catching's Theory of Relativity:

$$F + A = L$$

The more accomplished and brilliant you are, the more men (not all men, but most men) will be intrigued. If Miss Cashmere had just thrown a cheeky grin at Oprah's audience (or the bloke); if she'd just winked as if to say, "Oh, I know this stupid list of why I'm so intimidating is *impossible*," and laughed at herself, everybody would have loved her straightaway. She'd have given off a whiff of potent female charm. And there would have been hope.

I also suspect Miss Cashmere and some of the High Altitude Women at the McInerney party were blocking their opening courtship signals. Ma Nature went to a tinkly damn ton of trouble developing their androphonostic (man-slaying) skills—honing the suckers over the last 200 million years to guarantee chaps fall for them in the first few seconds. But these signals can get in the way of business, and so we get in the habit of blocking them. E.g., when a Miss High Altitude arrives in the conference room with the multibillionaire CEO and the VPs in their vivid yellow ties, what does she do? She insures she's not being "too feminine" by being a brass-busted twit. Anyway, I'll wager many of us are working overtime to throttle our inherited arts . . . or, at least . . . endeavoring to control our shimmy-shammy in "business situations."

Rutgers anthropologist Dr. Helen Fisher (the Empress of Research on the whole sexual-attraction/innate-courtship-behavior question) told me (as you no doubt remember from Part One) that the opening courtship signals are inborn.

"There is something called the coy look," said Dr. Fisher. "You cock your head and look up to the side and then look down and away—it's the characteristic courtship look. It's innate. Horses do it. Dogs do it. Human females do it. And it's very interesting how after a business meeting somebody will be embarrassed that they actually did some courtship gestures by mistake! I do think you learn to control these kinds of things and present yourself in a businesslike fashion."

I don't believe I'm throwing the Conair into the bathtub here when I posit that Miss Cashmere and the McInerney Women (including myself) (A) may have become so accustomed to batting down The Coy (and perhaps all opening courtship signals) in sales meetings, client gatherings, movie pitches, etc. that we are experiencing difficulty firing them off when we need them, and therefore (B) men are thinking about *us* what Tom Robbins once said:

"She has a mind like a steel trap and a vagina to match."

So let's wrap this up.

You scare the chaps? Excellent! You probably don't scare them enough. So for what remains of this week, pull off the veils—now don't lie there in bed reading *Mr. Right, Right Now!* with your bowl of popcorn (have you tried drizzling maple syrup over it when it's hot . . . *heaven!*) and pretend you don't know about the damn veils. I'm talking about the veils you hang between your "real" (i.e., powerful, intriguing) self and the actress "playing" the High Altitude Ball Thrasher (or the Timid Puss) you. The veils you hang in such profusion and thickness, in fact, men can't see through to the "true" you.

Man, my sentence structure is just going straight to hell, here. So this week yank 'em off. Give the beasts a taste of *all* the charms of your personality—your daring, your tenderness, your inquisitiveness, your rebelliousness, your spirituality, your cantankerousness, your impetuousness, your go-to-hell hilarity, your "goddess and your nymph" to paraphrase Willy Shakespeare. In other words, be yourself and you'll be *more* fabulous, *more* attractive; and please, don't go flapping your gums about what you "want in a man." It makes you look like you've spent too many long, torturous nights thinking about it.

DEAR E. JEAN: When should I go to bed with a guy? Do I wait till after three dates? After four dates? How am I supposed to know when it's "right"? I'm afraid to say NO because I don't want to lose a potential mate. But I'm afraid to say YES for obvious reasons.

—Crazed with Confusion

CRAZED, MY DEAR: You have managed to ask the single most useless and idiotic question known to woman. Let's give you the answer. Then we can bring *Mr. Right, Right Now!* to a swift conclusion and go out and have a party!

Week Six:
How to Mop Up the Floor
with Men

You know what happens now.

You've met a chap. He's handsome. He's rich. Lord! This makes a terrible story. You've heard it so often, yet it is the best story of all. You're wearing your Anna Sui turquoise minidress with your $15, marigold, plastic flip-flops and your five-inch-long garnet bead earrings and you're walking with the chap in the park eating cotton candy after a dinner of minestrone soup and vanilla ice cream with hot chocolate sauce (the chap had a chop), and the chap is looking at you with life-consuming passion, and lowering his voice, he says:

"Why don't we go back to my place?"

Or perhaps he says, "During dinner I ardently longed to rip that dress from your twisting torso." Either way . . . may we have a blast on the *Mr. Right, Right Now!* trumpet, please . . . we've arrived at the magic moment:

Bedding the Male Beast

Since, as Artie Schopenhauer says, "nothing less than the composi-tion of the next generation" is at stake here; since, in fact, the future of the human race to come hangs on your answer, the *last* thing Ma Nature wants is for you to stand in the blue-and-green park flashing your garnet earrings and mashing your cerebral cortex through a cheese grater, figuring out if this is your third date . . . or if you should count the time you ran into each other at the 50 Cent con-cert, so this would make it your fourth date . . . but if you subtract the time you had to leave the movie early because your boss called and asked you to fly to Houston, it would make it still the third date . . . but then if you added the time you spent together driving to the airport, it would be the fourth date.

"Dates" are for reality TV shows. Ma Nature doesn't *do* dates. Ma Nature does clicking and synchronizing and snogging and bond-ing and babies. That's it. So your answer to the chap's question is perfectly simple. *Viz,* have you clicked with him?

(A) If You Have *Not* Clicked . . . well, then, you are not synchronizing. And if you are not synchronizing, chances are high you will *never* synchronize. (You *do* remember Dr. Bernieri, don't you, Doll?) So if you are not synchronizing, and will never synchro-nize, it doesn't matter *when* you go to bed with the fellow, you will *never* end up as a couple anyway—so what the hell. If you fancy a romp in the begonias, say yes . . . and enjoy!

On the other hand . . .

(B) If You *Have* Clicked . . . there's an excellent chance you're synchronizing right now, and if you're synchronizing right now, that means all is well, and if all is well, that means things couldn't be better, and if things couldn't be better, then you are a couple *already,* so what the hell. If you'd love a begonia romp, say yes . . . and enjoy!

I sense your astonishment.

I assure you, Doll . . .

Man Catching Law #15
A Man Catcher Is Free to Romp in the Begonias
Whenever She Pleases.

You are free. Free. Free. Free. Free. Free. Free. Free. Free. Free. Free. Free. Free. Free. Free. Free. [Note to editor, David Hirshey: Can we have the word "free" printed for an entire page?] From now on you can forget what men want. You can do what *you* want. You can be yourself. You are either synchronizing with the chap or you are not synchronizing with the chap. (And if your *are* synchronizing with the chap, enjoying a romp in the begonias together will only enhance and deepen your feelings for each other.)

And as for that platitudinous, money-sucking advice-book malarkey about "holding off" to increase the chap's desire . . . har! Now I realize I advised this myself in Chapter Four, but there is not one scrap of evidence showing that a modern American woman who "holds off" will get herself snapped into the $9,500 Vera Wang wedding number faster, better, or more often than a woman who jumps right into the begonias. Repeat. Not a shred of proof.[1]

---

1. Yours truly is, of course, not alone in pointing this out. Natalie Angier, the brilliant Pulitzer-winning science writer for *The New York Times,* whom yours truly worships, says in her stupendous book *Woman: An Intimate Geography,* "But where is the evidence that women who 'give in too easily' do not get married, while those who remain chaste do?" If Natalie can't find the evidence, *nobody* can.

But you have a major question:

What about that dark-haired, velvet-eyed VP of sales you went out with last year and had a "great" time, went out with again, had a "great" time, went out with a third time, leapt into bed, had a "great" time, and you never heard from him again—what about that?

I submit to you that you did not click in the first place.

Clicking does not happen every day, ya know. Week Four lists so many places to meet because it's paramount you bump into large numbers of high-caliber men. Why? Because Ma Nature is choosy, choosy, choosy, when it comes to causing you to click with a fellow. The click is precious. The click is powerful. (If you've ever clicked with a married man and had the very devil of a time getting out of it, you know how potent the click can be.) Ma Nature has been perfecting the click for 200 million years because she wants her pretty new gene-combinations; and she will drag your shapely bottom through the fire and ices of hell to bring you, breathless, raging-haired, and feisty, to Click City. That did *not* happen with Mr. Velvet Eyes.

I submit to you the "great" times you experienced with Velvet happened because you went to lovely restaurants, your short, green tulle skirt received admiring glances, your new haircut made you look better than Cameron Diaz, and you drank a bottle of Cristal.

But Beware the Chastity Belt— Bible Belt Bull Hockey

You can click with a fellow; but he may be a fellow who believes a woman should "hold off" for religious/philosophic/masculinist-centered flapdoodle. The poor chap may not even know he believes this. Hell's bells, the poor bastard may believe he believes exactly the opposite. If you invite *this* fellow for the begonia romp too early in the game (or if he keeps nudging you toward the begonia patch and you "give in" and say yes), he'll go for it, he'll revel in it, yes; but it will boil his brains and it could blow your whole synchronization deal right out of the water.

(*Note:* Rent Hitchcock's *Notorious* and watch Cary Grant come unhinged over Ingrid Bergman. It is one of the sublime movies and one of the finest demonstrations of how the "Clicking—Oop! She's A Slut!" deal works.)

But here is the good news. Since you do not know beforehand whether the fellow is this kind of fellow, and since even the fellow may not know he is this kind of fellow, again, be yourself, do as you please. Enjoy!

The Man Catching Caveat

(The Only Such Dire Warning in *Mr. Right, Right Now!*)

It is your attitude *after* sex that is key. If you are clingy and whiny and burst into racking sobs and try to mess with the bloke's head, forget it. If you are a Man Catcher down to the tips of your Donna Karan bedroom slippers . . . if you stretch on the Porthault like a tigress and demand he go fetch you oranges, then everything's cool, and the male beast will desire you even more madly.

So that's it, Doll. Be yourself. [Hirshey, my darling, could we have "be yourself" fill the rest of the page? If the lovely reader is not herself the whole Man Catching Theory flies out the door.] Nothing could be simpler. If you place yourself where there are high numbers of men, it is a *mathematical certainty* you will meet several lovely beasts. Then Ma Nature, who has created you as a veritable mantrap, excuse the plain English, will see to it that you attract a chap, that you click, and that you synchronize. And if you are synchronizing, all you have to do is be yourself and keep doing what you are doing. And if you are yourself and keep doing what you're doing, you will roar straight through the engagement (if that is what you want), up the aisle, down into your dream house, over to the hospital for your first child, and so on and so forth, until death do you part . . . or until the chap starts acting like a jerkball, whichever comes first.

The point is, the Man Catching Theory gives you a powerful foundation on which to build something *marvelous*. So, Doll, I wish you now melodious adieu. It's been delicious spending these last six weeks with . . . whoa!

Aphrodite: Move over, moron. Thou screweth up this book.

E: Ye gods, Goddess! Uh . . . Er, I'm not sure how to address Your Highness, Your Goddess-ship. You . . . are, you're the, uh, the Goddess of Desire? Right? You make us mortals lose our brains? Make us run around falling in love with each other? That's you?

Aphrodite: Thou puny twat!

(Aphrodite, who has suddenly appeared in my parlor in a swirl of foam and shells, turns her aquamarine eyes on me, and sparks fly from—well, I'm not sure from where . . . her hair? Her forehead? Most likely she expects me to faint. She is—I can say without exaggeration—the most beautiful creature I have ever laid eyes on in my life. A thousand times more ravishing than Halle Berry. Does that describe it? Aphrodite goes about six foot six, wears a bloodred Donatella Versace and little strappy, gold Christian Leboutin sandals from which her toes peek like dainty mushrooms. Indeed, wherever she treads, flowers spring up in my carpet. There is also a live dove in her hair, and my dogs—who always jump on visitors, pin them against the doorjamb, and attempt to have sex with them—immediately lie down at Aphrodite's feet and turn their eyes up at her in total adoration.)

Aphrodite: Thou hast *not* finished with *Mr. Right, Rightest Now!*

E: No? Well . . . I'm delighted that you . . . would you take a seat, please, O Lady? May I bring you a—

Aphrodite: Taketh this dictation, thou half-wit.

E: Well . . . of course, my pleasure, Lady.

Aphrodite: Thou wert wrong about thy begonia-romping.

E: Listen, before you start on how wrong I was—I beg your pardon, Lady, but you're not planning on making me irresistible are you?

Aphrodite: Type!

E: You see, I have to get this chapter done today, ya know. And I don't have time to become any more attractive.

Aphrodite: Type, sow teat!

E: Yes, Lady. But for goddess's sakes, watch those sparks.

(With a disdainful glance around the room, Aphrodite puts a hand on her shapely hip, which juts out like Brazil, and, shaking back her ankle-length hair, pauses a moment to ruminate.)

Aphrodite: If a mortal woman—type! If a mortal female wanteth a man to falleth for her, she must weareth his nerves to *shreds* in suspense. *Shreds!* The Male Muttonheads must beggeth for the smallest favor!

E: But research shows, excuse me, Lady, the research—

Aphrodite: Pegasus crap on thy "research!"

E: But . . .

Aphrodite: Type! The longer a Muttonhead is madeth to coolest his heels, the harder and further he fallest.

E: Now, now, Lady. Let's not go telling the Lovely Reader, whom I adore, to start behaving like a dim-witted spinster from the 1950s—

Aphrodite: Wilt thou apply thy fat fingers to thy iMac, or shall I smite thine underwear drawer and turneth thy silken lingerie to snotrags!

E: You can't—I beg your pardon, Lady—you can't tell the Lovely Reader to be a "tease."

Aphrodite: Minotaur Fart! Every mortal woman hath the *instinct* of a tantalizer. It runneth in her blood like wine. Speaketh of which, hath thou no nectar?

(I cease taking dictation, go to the refrigerator, return, and sacrifice to the goddess two six-packs of Guinness.)

Aphrodite (downing three bottles, and burping): Women art more interested in sex than the Muttonheads, anywayest.

E: Yes, indeed. A toast! Women *are* more interested in sex. Well, thanks for dropping by, Your Highness. I have to print your dictation now and drive the manuscript to HarperCollins.

Aphrodite: Nay! Thou's book canst not end. Thou must telleth the Mortal Reader how to weddeth the Muttonhead.

E: No, Lady. *Landing* a chap is one thing. It's based on primal forces. Clicking, synchronizing, and so on. But marriage? Har! Men invented marriage. And, frankly, they can keep it.

Aphrodite (opening the second six-pack and draining two bottles): But the Mortal Woman not feeleth she getteth her drachma's worth.

E: No, Lady. The Mortal Woman should be very suspicious of anyone who tells her "how" to get married. Each Mortal Woman is unique. And each one of her chaps is unique. There's no single strategy that works. I'd have to confer with each individual. The best thing is what I said earlier: if the Lovely Reader is synchronizing with the chap she loves, she should just be herself and continue doing what she's doing. It will lead to what she wants.

Aphrodite: Fie! Fie! At least telleth the Mortal Reader not to rompest in the begonias with the Muttonhead until the Muttonhead rolleth on the linoleum and sweareth he loveth the Mortal Reader.

E: I disagree, Lady.

Aphrodite: Zazz! And whenst *thou's* worshiped as the Goddess of Desire *thou* canst dictate to a moron. Now, offereth me more sacrifices.

E: I'll make us a stack of peanut butter and Fluff sandwiches, how's that?

Aphrodite (festively throwing the last bottle through my living room window): And bringeth me four hogsheads of macaroni and cheese. I tireth of speaking of men.

Farewell, Lovely Reader

Good-bye, Doll!

My! How fast the time has gone. Six weeks! I've had such a delicious time, I wish we didn't have to part.

What'd you say?

Oh. Your new fiancé is asking you to close the book? He wants you to turn off the light and come to bed? Just tell him, "In a minute, Moose Balls, you darling! I'm just reading the last sentence of *Mr. Right, Right Now!* and then E. Jean wants me to give you a big kiss!"

Oop!

Could you please switch the light back on, Doll?

Thanks.

This won't take a moment. I just want to alert you to a momentous—a *stunning!*—discovery that's reported today on the front page of *The New York Times*. The differences between men and women are much (oh, much!) greater than previously thought.

Yes.

The genomes of humans and chimpanzees match right down the line—our genes and chimps genes are 98.5% identical. The genomes of men and women match, uh, only about 98%.

That means *you*, an elegant human female, have more in common with a female chimpanzee than you do with a human male.

Explains a lot, doesn't it?

Until this discovery, of course everybody thought male-female differences were due to sex hormones. Ha! There's considerably more going on. "The reality is," says Dr. David C. Page, leader of the team of researchers at the Whitehead Institute in Cambridge, Massachusetts, which announced the finding, "the genetic differ-

ence between males and females absolutely dwarfs all other differences in the human genome."

Indeed, we're so different, the miracle is that men and women
ever get together, let alone get together long enough to have sex to
make more men and women.

Now it's clear why Ma Nature forces the chaps to fall for you so
quickly, isn't it? If you didn't arrive on the scene *loaded* with inborn
attractors . . . if the mere *sight* of you didn't cause a fellow's
dopamine circuits to start firing . . . if you both didn't feel that
"click," why, Doll, you'd have a better chance at a beautiful friendship with Miss Chimpy Lips than with a man.

I think it may also explain (at least partly) why men and women
break up so quickly.

Ma Nature is interested in pushing you together to get her fancy
gene-combinations—not in *keeping* you together. So you and the
beau may start out wildly enamored, then discover you possess so
little in common it's a torment to stay together. This is not to say you
and a man *can't* enjoy a world-shattering, unnamed, untamed, everlasting love affair . . . or an exceptionally happy friendship; I'm just
saying this 98% thing makes it difficult for some of us.

Bearing that in mind, I've drawn up—Lord! I loathe ending *Mr.
Right, Right Now!* like this, but it's an emergency—certain facts
must be pointed out, cautions given. Crashing fellows into your
arms without alerting you in advance to particular pitfalls would be
criminal. May my left eyebrow be ripped from my head if I don't
properly forewarn you!

So. Now. You know *The 119 Best Places To* **Find** *The Male
Beast*, not to mention how to land him once you've found him, it is
now imperative that you ponder:

The 79 Best Ways to LOSE the Male Beast

Best *Way #1. Always end arguments by turning some deeply private secret he's confided to you . . . against him. Then add, "Screw you, you slobbering half-wit!"*

#2. Beg him to read your journal.

#3. Don't mince words. If he asks, reply, "Why, yes, dear, now that I look at it, your penis is the smallest I've ever seen in my life."

#4. You know you shouldn't call him too much, so say to yourself, "I'm an adult. He's an adult. I refuse to play stupid games."

#5. Call him repeatedly.

#6. If he doesn't call back, e-mail him. If he doesn't return your e-mail, fax him a funny little joke. If he still doesn't call, drop by his office and surprise him with a "cute" card. If he's not at his office, drive to his house, wait for him at his front door, and, when he arrives, tell him he can do anything he wants with you.

#7. *Ask him once a week, "So, where do we stand?"*

#8. *Or, if you prefer a more dramatic scrotum-tightener, ask, "So, where do we stand <u>as a couple</u>?"*

#9. *Just happen to have tickets to a play. Convince yourself the man loves plays. Call him and say, "I have two tickets to Frozen Eggs where the actress harvests her eggs onstage and delivers a fascinating monologue about it!" Whatever you do, don't have tickets to anything exciting like a play-<u>OFF</u>.*

#10. *Rarely wear high heels to bed.*

#11. *Be the first woman in recorded history to actually tell a man exactly how many chaps she's slept with.*

#12. *Every time he makes a joke, roll your eyes and say, "Very funny. Ha ha."*

#13. *Count the number of days since the last time you saw him. Get so freaked-out about the number of days since the last time you saw him, spend all the time when you actually see him telling him there's been too much time since the last time you saw him and you think he'd see you more often if he only got to know the "real" you.*

#14. *He may not <u>want</u> to know about the real you, but never mind. Keep telling him about the real you anyway. Chase him down the street if necessary, claw at his trousers if you must, but by all means, keep telling him all about the real you.*

#15. *Make him watch the Ya-Ya Sisterhood.*

#16. *Fixate on the future. Focus on his taking you to the Bahamas for Valentine's Day.*

#17. *If he does not take you to the Bahamas for Valentine's Day, act real light and breezy and then suddenly collapse in a heap, burst into tears, and inform him he has "intimacy issues."*

#18. *Speaking of which, always cry after sex.*

#19. *Better yet, cry during sex.*

#20. *Criticize his mother.*

#21. *Borrow $2,300 from him.*

#22. *Maintain a ladylike air of dignified seriousness when snogging.*

#23. *Ask him about his "personal feelings concerning the relationship" while he's watching the final two minutes of the seventh game of the NBA championship series. If he doesn't hear you, snap off the TV and hurl the remote out the window.*

#24. *He'll refuse to speak to you after you've hurled the remote out the window, but so what? This is an excellent opportunity to confront him about his "fear of being inferior."*

#25. *Do you own an old pair of baggy maroon sweatpants? Wear them.*

#26. *Every night.*

#27. *Blind yourself to his faults. (Of course, if you happen to see a fault by mistake, immediately point it out to him.)*

#28. *Is he feeling a tad overwhelmed by the serious turn your affair is taking? Surprise him with loads of expensive gifts for no reason.*

#29. *Say sweetly, "Either your idiot dog goes . . . or I go."*

#30. *Withhold sex for two weeks.*

#31. *In the first month of your affair, tell him you love riding in his Jeep with the top down. In the second month, tell him you sometimes like the top up, but you love all the windows down. In the third month, tell him to roll the top and the windows up, or he can stick his frickin' Jeep up his frickin' . . . (you get the picture).*

#32. *Don't pay back the $2,300.*

#33. *Make complicated plans for the two of you to spend lots and lots and lots of time with your parents.*

#34. *Nag.*
Nag.
Nag.
Nag.
Nag.

#35. *Wear his favorite shirt without asking and spill Cherry Coke on it while driving his new Lexus, which you accidentally crash into the car in front of you at a stoplight.*

#36. *Wrap your whole life around him.*

#37. *Reassure him that all men, uh, have, uh, difficulties in the sack, but not to worry—you've discussed his problem with his friends, and they all think it's hilarious.*

#38. *Giggle at his receding hairline.*

#39. *When he calls you at your office to say he loves you and that he's going to go shoot baskets with the guys after work, inform him, "No, Humpfart. The only shooting going on will*

be me shooting you if you don't take that Pilates class with
me at seven!"

#40. Keep pestering him to explain what the Matrix is—in the
middle of it.

#41. Stop shaving your legs, except when you shave your legs for
"special occasions," and then use his new razor.

#42. When he asks you and your kids to attend a religious service
at his church/synagogue/mosque, snicker and say, "Please.
Your religion is a form of child abuse."

#43. Tell him oral sex makes you gag . . . except when he does it.

#44. Believe he won't mind if you've gained 37 pounds.

#45. When he's conducting an important client presentation, call
him with an "emergency." When he comes on the line, tell
him excitedly that your psychic just told you that you and he
were married in a former life in 16th-century Scotland, and
that you're destined to be together forever and ever and ever
and ever!

#46. Festering resentment. Try it.

#47. Continue to hold the opinion "men are babies."

#48. Never tell him he makes you happy. Never say that sometimes you're so proud to be with him you want to weep for
joy.

#49. Drink too much at a party and vomit on his shoes.

#50. Inform him that his five-year-old daughter "needs to see a
therapist" because she refused to kiss you hello.

#51. *Never cook <u>anything</u> for him.*

#52. *Refer to his car as "a piece of shit."*

#53. *Don't let him miss you. (I.e., spend every blessed moment with/near/on/under/over him—particularly those blessed moments when you feel bloated and paranoid.)*

#54. *Let him miss you too much. Rarely come home from the office till after 10:30 P.M.*

#55. *Invite your most attractive girlfriends over to play croquet.*

#56. *When dining with friends, if he begins talking about his dream of taking poor, underprivileged kids sailboating, snort and tell him he's "full of crap."*

#57. *Get old. (I don't mean chronologically.)*

#58. *Keep yourself informed about his activities. Call around to his friends and check up on him. When he walks in the door, sniff him over like you're a pit bull looking for a Quarter-Pounder.*

#59. *Make him take the quizzes in Ladies' Mags.*

#60. *Explain that if primal man could learn to walk upright in a mere 2 million years, a moron like him can walk to the incinerator with the garbage.*

#61. *Make him go to couples therapy with you if his LMQS (Ladies' Mag Quiz Score) is lower than your sister's boyfriend's.*

#62. *Act like the challenge before you is not to become someone, but to become someone's wife.*

#63. *Rarely be in a playful mood.*

#64. *You know everything there is to know about him, so just smile and mentally plan the outfit you're wearing tomorrow while he's talking.*

#65. *Never have your wallet with you.*

#66. *Trick him, dupe him, deceive him with every breath you take—i.e., follow* The Rules.

#67. *When you're at a formal dance and you bump into an old beau, throw your arms around the beau's neck, hold your pelvis against his, and squeal, "Oh, God! Oh, God!"*

#68. *When you run out of things to fight about, invite his mother over to help you "organize" his closets.*

#69. *Recently met the man of your dreams on-line? When you meet him in person, bring along the sweater you've knit for him.*

#70. *Refuse to tie him up and play Slaveboy and Empress because it may "put wrinkles in your good scarves."*

#71. *Spend as much time with your hair and makeup as you need . . . particularly when <u>he's</u> waiting in the car to take you to dinner with his boss.*

#72. *If he's experiencing career difficulties (see #71), gently point out that when he loses this job, he'll probably never get another one.*

#73. *If you went to a better college than he did, never let him forget it.*

#74. *If you're worried he'll discover how "unlikable" you are once he gets to know you, start acting really, really obnoxious right now.*

#75. *After going out four times, instruct your children to call him Daddy—even if they are over 25.*

#76. *If you earn more money than he does, make sure you boost his ego by letting him pay for absolutely everything.*

#77. *When you're driving home from a party, refer to every single woman he talked to as "a famous slut."*

#78. *Take yourself very very very seriously.*

#79. *Let him know that <u>every</u> day is Judgment Day as far as you and he are concerned and that you'd rather be right than happy.*

Well.

Egads.

That's done. Whew. Lord! Look at the time! Must dress! There's a party tonight—an exceedingly posh, foul one—a veritable hive of writers, movie stars, politicians, prominent and extremely beautiful people, and so on, and it so happens I possess an exceptionally charming new dress with gold spangles around the hem—so must fly, Doll! Will drop *Mr. Right, Right Now!* off at HarperCollins, and then nothing but dissipation and mandarin martinis . . . so, again, I embrace you, I kiss you, I bid you melodious adieu!

Wait—

Am I forgetting something? What else is there to say? Oh, that 98% business about having more in common with female chimpanzees than human males . . .

It's good to know. But, really, love doesn't love laws, now does it? And you *can* make love last. How? Preserve your mystery. And if you've clicked with a man, all (all!) you must do is follow . . .

Man Catching Law #16
If You Like a Lad,
and He Likes You,
Just Keep On Doing . . .
What You Do.

Keep doing what you're doing, Doll, *do what works, and don't do what doesn't work.* Simple as that! So, here's old E. Jean wishing you health, happiness, and worshipful hordes of handsome lovers!

P.S. I also have a stunning dress, Armani, pale blue, perfect for wearing to a ceremony, so I'd appreciate a wedding invitation, ya know.

Afterword:
The 6-Day Plan

Guide to Enjoying This Appendage

1. Doll, this afterword is an accident.

2. It's only here because the producers at *The CBS Early Show* decide to put two comely Manhattan career women—Traci and Lirone—on camera and follow them through the *6-Week Plan*. "We'll *test* your claim, E. Jean," says Nanci Ross, senior producer at CBS, "and see if a couple of smart women really *can* land their dream men in six weeks."

3. Nanci's left eyelash tells me Nanci thinks it's complete bullshit. But so what? I'm ... *ecstatic*. Julie Chen! Hannah Storm! Harry What's-His-Name! Hair! Makeup! Bagels in the greenroom! Six outfits! Lord! I nearly go distracted.

4. Thirteen days into the shoot I ascertain my own personal ass is grassed. The basis of *M.R.R.N.!* is science. Traci and Lirone turn out to be human. Not to say Traci and Lirone aren't just *brimful* of charm, brains, wiles, allurements, not to mention Beyoncé-grade upper thighs, and so on. We start by shooting Traci and Lirone at The Night of 26 Men at the posh Bryant Park Hotel Cellar Bar (*viz:* Traci, Lirone, and 26 handsome devils). Next we shoot Traci and Lirone in preposterously sexy (but sporty!) outfits at the batting cages in the Chelsea Piers Sports Center (*viz:* Traci, Lirone, and 400 doctors, lawyers, investment bankers, etc., etc.).

5. Traci and Lirone don't like *any* of them.

6. Cut to: Grand Central Station. I make Traci and Lirone go up to 20 handsome strangers, start conversations ("Oh! I love your haircut! Excuse me. No, no. I mean really. I'm not kidding. I want my brother to have that cut. *Sweet!*" or whatever the moment offers), and then collect their phone numbers. Aside from those gregarious showboats on *The Apprentice,* most people would prefer jumping out of a plane to addressing a total stranger. Not Traci. Traci possesses panache out the bazoo. Traci's hair is the color of iodine. She has a saucy wardrobe. She could give two flying figs what men "think" of her. (Or actually, she *does* care what they think, but not really.) She breezes through Grand Central—CBS crew loping behind her—asking one chap where to get a cheeseburger, admiring a second fellow's briefcase, inquiring of a third if he has change for a $50 bill, and so on. Phone numbers just *hail* down upon her. Lirone, on the other hand, turns pale, cramps up, and lapses into a sort of dismal coma. She *expects* to get screwed over.

7. Cut to: Man sitting behind a newspaper having his shoes shined.

"Ask him how much you should tip the shoeshine man," I tell Lirone.

I nudge her toward him with my elbow.

"I can't," says Lirone, clasping the sleeve of my coat.

"You *can*."

"I can't."

"You *can*."

"Can't."

"You can, really now, *come on*."

"Umph."

"Come on."

"Umphmm."

Riveting television.

She goes up to him at last.

"Excuse me," she says, in a fidgety, skittish voice, "I hate to bother you, but but but but—"

The man puts down his paper. He's just *unmercifully* good-looking.

"But . . . I . . . I . . ." says Lirone. Suddenly, she ceases twisting her frozen hands together. His beauty so stuns her, she forgets to be self-conscious. (Thank you, Ma Nature!) "I was wondering, how much should I tip if I decide to have my boots shined?"

The man smiles at her.

"A dollar." He looks at her boots. They are well-polished and sheen darkly. "Or two," he says, raising his eyes up past her tight-fitting lilac sweater set to her flushed face.

"Thanks," says Lirone.

She turns. Softly the man's smile fades as he watches her walk away.

The entire exchange takes about nine seconds, not counting the shoe shiner offering to do her boots for *half off*.

"Go back!" I whisper. "The man likes you!"

"Huh?"

"He likes you! Go back! Go back!"

She goes back.

8. They go out to dinner. A delicious evening! He leaves for Europe or the Caribbean (I can't recall) the next day on a long business trip. Shoeshine Guy is Hannah Storm's fave on *The Early Show*.

Does this little exercise at Grand Central help Lirone and Traci? You bet. It builds Lirone's confidence. She's thunderstruck that every single man reacts to her with a smile. (A couple of guys refuse to talk, but it's because of the CBS cameras.) It reframes Lirone's thinking. It also forces both Traci and Lirone to meet men in such high numbers it becomes mathematically possible to make the acquaintance of a fellow who doesn't make them want to barf. And since the conversations are brief—"I like your shirt"—but not too brief (i.e., just long enough to know if there's a liking), and since they're compelled to be in close physical proximity to exchange numbers (i.e., his DNA can read her DNA, and vv), clicking can occur. (And if you're guessing the 20 Handsome Strangers are going to be a part of the 6-Day Plan, you're right.)

9. So back to the question: Do Lirone and Traci land their dream men in 6 weeks?

10. Traci and The Musician meet at a salon party early on, and fall head over ears between Week Three and Week Four. He is, without exaggeration, the laidest-back guy to ever appear on morning television. During his and Traci's cooking-date segment, he stands with his hands in his pockets, lolling against the stove, moving only his eyeballs. But the look on his face is bordering on heavenly bliss.

11. Lirone and *her* cooking-date-segment guy, The Hunky Editor, whom she meets in Week Four on GreatBoyfriends.com, chase each other around the kitchen, laughing and chopping, eggs excitedly breaking in every direction. Lirone, who is usually sheet-white—everyone in her family is a doctor; she herself is a psychiatric social worker—sits down at the table to eat. Her color is high. Her hair is rowdily tumbled. She leans toward The Editor to fuss with something on his plate. The Editor seizes her around the waist. Lirone emits a low-pitched silvery chime of laughter. And America witnesses The First Kiss.

12. Yes. Lirone is nearly the death of me. By the time we reach Week Six, Lirone can't decide between two men: The Hunky Editor (tall, funny, sexy, brilliant) and The Finance Guy (handsome, smooth; but I personally suspect he's a bounder and whenever I watch them together I throb at the temples). Lirone goes unslept, unfed, unbrushed, trying to decide between them. In fact, I don't even think Lirone knows which man she wants until she walks into the CBS Fifth Avenue studios and announces her decision to Hannah live on the air.

13. It's The Hunky Editor.

14. Thank God.

15. So. Take the sizzling success of the *6-Week Plan*, couple it with the Numbers-from-Handsome-Strangers, and add the final element:

16. An over-caffeinated audience in Seattle. I'm giving a so-called reading in a bookstore. Intense public yawning greets my whole 6-week deal. Apparently Seattle women don't *have* six weeks. "Well . . ." I say. "I don't see why we can't do this in six *days*." That perks up the Pendletons. Of course I haven't the foggiest idea *what* the Six Days are, I just sort of flap my gums, collapse each week into a day, mix it up, toss in the collecting of phone numbers, the bookstore gives away free wine, I sign 88 books, leave for Toronto, and forget all about it. A week later I start getting e-mails. *Damn.* The 6-Day Plan is *fly*!

17. So . . . though nobody *needs* a man, or even *wants* a man 87% of the time, here's the 6-Day Plan:

18. Wait.

19. A bit of pregame prep is in order.

Look, Doll, basically what you'll be doing for the next few days is going where there are high numbers of men. And because going to where there are high numbers of the buggers won't do any good unless you're beguiling, you'll be given something to be beguiling about. And that something is getting numbers and taking photographs of good-looking guys. I know, I know, it sounds ridiculous, but it works! Getting a photograph gives you an excuse to spark something. And when you spark something—well, you remember the *Snow White Effect* (i.e., if a fellow likes the way you look, he will like you; if he likes you, he will find you intelligent and intriguing; if he finds you intelligent and intriguing, he'll feel energized, exhilarated, and sexy; if he feels energized, exhilarated, and sexy—and you like him—you'll synchronize; and when you synchronize, that is a chap who's *crushing* on you, big time). But first you gotta spark it.

If you lack cunning, if you'd rather walk seven miles in a pair of tight Chanel pumps than speak to a strange man, here's how you do it: Simply saunter up and say, "Excuse me, hi, hello, I'm (Your Enthralling Name). I know this sounds weird but I'm on special assignment for this lunatic columnist at *Elle* magazine. She's assigned me the task of shooting a picture (show your Polaroid/digital camera) and getting the number of every hot guy I see. Yeah, yeah, she's a moron; but it's turning out to be quite an entertaining little experiment. Because at the end of the week, my job is to choose the most seriously handsome man and take him out to dinner." If that doesn't start a conversation, nothing will. Then, of course, snap his picture, get his number, give him *your* number, and when you arrive home, tape all the pictures you've collected that day up on the wall.

Want to know why *else* you're getting the numbers and photos? Obviously it's a genius way to meet guys. But mainly it's because the women who succeed at the 6-Day Plan are the women who *expect* to succeed. Therefore I advise you to **A)** take a friend along the first couple of days. (If you're a bit shy, you can't do this on your own.) **B)** Clear all the losers from your life for the week— you don't want any Black Hole Numbskulls sucking your energy. And **C)** set the small goal of just getting the number/photograph (i.e., *not* the goal of Finding The Love Of Your Life). According to the book *Confidence*, the brilliant Harvard Business School professor Rosabeth Moss Kanter argues that small wins lead to greater confidence; greater confidence leads to the belief you can succeed; and when you believe you'll succeed, you *will* meet Mr. Right.

OK. Let's serve this thing up while it's still vibrating:

Day One (Saturday)

Morning:
- Send e-mails to 30 guys you like on Match, J-Date, Nerve, or GreatBoyfriends.

Afternoon:
- Rent a scooter. Flash around town on the bugger. Wear a skirt. Screech up to the stoplight, look over at the guy in the Porsche. Give him a smile and say, "Ai—ight! When this light turns green I'm going to tromp this thing and blow you away!"
- Collect 10 numbers/pictures.

Evening:
- What's goin' on? Are the Yankees/49ers/ Blackhawks/Rockets playing? Is there an Usher concert? Poetry slam? Jazz festival? Charity dance? Can you score tickets? No? Then put on your tightest dress, load up on the perfume, slip on your shades, pick up your best friend (on the scooter preferably), and roll like a bitch to the hip bowling alley. (If bowling's not hot in your town yet, go to the dodgeball court. Dodgeball not happenin'? Go to a drag race, or the motocross track.) Rouse the boys into a libido-jangling stud frenzy.
- Pocket 10 numbers/photos.

Late Evening:
- Preposterously hot club.
- You're good for two more numbers/photos, right?
- Return e-mails to guys you heard back from, and suggest meeting for coffee.

- Tape 22 pictures to wall. (If you have the time, print out the pictures of the Internet guys and put those up as well.)

Note: I don't know why (just going by what the women who've tested this thing tell me) there's a slightly better than 50% chance you'll meet the guy you like best on this first day.

Day Two (Sunday)
Morning:
- Church.
- Not churchy? Volunteer at Habitat for Humanity.
- Pray for five numbers. Nail five photographs.

Afternoon:
- Golf course.
- Nine holes.
- No handicap here: get five numbers/five pictures.

Evening:
- Dinner at hot sports bar.
- Order three baskets of French fries. Gorge on a plate of half a dozen pictures/photos. (Men love women who *eat*.)

Late Evening:
- Pool hall or cigar bar.
- Rack up four numbers/pictures.
- Return e-mails to guys. Set coffee dates for Tuesday.
- Tape 20 new photos to wall.

Note: You'll meet a couple of men who'll be so smitten with you and your camera and your numbers and your whole fascinating trip, they'll immediately ask you out. If they're appealing, go. But explain that you're on a strict and compact timetable; and then either take them along on your next task, or make the date for *after* your scheduled activities. This will cause the right fellows to break into paroxysms of hankering.

Day Three (Monday)

Morning:
- Sleep late.
- Hair appointment.

Afternoon:
- Drop off cookies at fire station.
- Lunch at a male bastion (doesn't matter which).
- Burn calories getting five numbers/five photos.
- Work.
- Sit on a giant blue ball/set more coffee dates with Internet guys.

Note: Yes, you should probably alert the boss you're "working on a personal project" and won't be around much. Promise to make up for it next week.

Evening:
- 6:30 rock-climbing.
- Scramble five numbers/photos.
- 9:00 dinner at hot restaurant. Sit at the bar. Order the $14 chocolate martini and a plate of whatever kind of salad has nine colors, five numbers/five pictures.

Late Evening:
- Karaoke bar.
- Note three numbers/three shots.
- Tape 18 handsome pictures to wall.

Day Four (Tuesday)

Morning:
- Sleep late.
- Makeup appointment.

Afternoon:

- Lunch in the park. (If it's raining, sit under a pink umbrella.)
- Entice 10 numbers/photos. (You'll be looking *that* good!)

Early Evening:

- 6:00–8:30 coffee dates.
- If you meet somebody charming, go on to dinner. If not . . .
- Arrive late for lecture on quantum physics.
- If you don't get two numbers/photos, perhaps you *already* got four in an alternate universe.
- 10:30 set up easel and paint. Yes, it's the middle of the night. *That's what makes it interesting.* (I don't need to tell you to choose the busiest street, do I?)
- Sketch six numbers/photos.
- Tape eighteen new photographs to wall.

Note to anybody who's wigging out: Look, I know you're not doing half this stuff. But getting these photos/numbers is the coolest single activity ever. If you stick with it, you'll meet enough chaps to last a lifetime (or for three months at least).

Day Five (Wednesday)

Morning:

- Sleep late. Study pictures in bed. Select your eight faves. Include the Internet guys you like best. Call and invite everyone over for a poker party tonight at your house.

Afternoon—into Evening:

- Buy honey BRQ chips, pretzels, beer, etc. Borrow round poker table. Suffer near-death experience trying to stay out of chips till 8:30. Clean house. Make sandwiches. Haul in the *Cincinnati Kid*–type lighting. When the doorbell rings, answer it wearing something orgasmic.

Evening:

- You and six men. (It's impossible that *all* eight will be able to make it.)
- The object of the poker party is to decide whom you like. By jamming a half-dozen ardent, horny fellows around a table, you'll force them into a hot, primal competition, and when chaps compete, you become *more* desirable in their eyes, more lovely, more hot, more rad.
- Here are your tasks for the evening: Torment them! Vex them! Thrash them!
  1. You will glance entrancingly at one lad, while putting a pretzel into the mouth of another lad.
  2. Instead of answering when a chap asks you a question, you will reply with a smile and silence . . . then you will glance away and speak to another man. (*Lethal* when employed at the right time, i.e., just when a chap craves your attention.)
  3. You were *born* to be brilliant at these tasks.
  4. You will whisper in a bloke's ear. It will cause the bloke to lean close to you. Your breath will feel warm on his cheek. He will smell your animal scent. And just when he's *caught, that's* when you draw away and, with magnificent indifference, start talking about the Lakers.
  5. During the shuffle, you will catch a fellow's attention and wink at him. He will be stunned, unsure if it's meant for him, and just when he's about to react, you'll swivel your body away and shift your attention to another fellow. This will throw the first fellow completely off balance.
  6. You will run *all* the lads over the hot coals of anticipation; but at some point you'll zero in on your favorite. You'll bring him a cupcake. You'll stand behind his chair. You'll tell him casually he's the "luckiest man in the room."

7. This will amp the other fellows to near madness.

Day Six (Thursday)

- Wake at noon. Stretch like a tigress. Retrieve 133 text messages from your poker players. I don't have to spell out the rest, do I, Doll?

After . . . the Afterword

How to Land a Man in 6 Hours

Of course, if you don't want to spend six weeks or six days or six anything . . . if you're a lagging kumquat and just want a male beast delivered to you . . . fine. I'll send him to you myself.

In fact, I'll deliver to you 27 incredibly handsome possibilities. Yes! Just go to Catch27.com. It's my new Web site where you get 27 hot Catches, and then (because I know you're picky) you TRADE the ones you don't want . . . just like baseball cards. It's a hoot, and it's my present to you for buying this book.

Thanks!

I would be nobody without:

David Hirshey
Megan Newman
Jane Friedman
Alex Postman
Michael Solomon
Robbie Myers
Shelby Meizlik
Jennifer Swihart
Kate Stark
Katie Couric
Cande Carroll
Tom Robbins
Stephanie Drachkovitch
Marilyn Johnson
Carol Martin

Jesse Kornbluth

George Clooney

Nanci Ross

Oprah Winfrey

Karen Collins

Lila Haber

Andrea Brown

Leah Carlson-Stanisic

Rob Fleder

Tom Carroll III

Ginia Bellafante

Miss Squire

Greg Talenfeld

Danielle Mattoon

Melanie Rock

Joe Terry

Barbara Carroll

Sarah Lazin

Nick Trautwein

David Quammen

Beth Tilson

Roger Ailes

Hannah Storm

Joanne Mazzella

Tom Carroll

Betty Carroll

Matt Lauer

TO THE PUBLISHER

If there are any foul-ups, gaffes, or errors in this so-called book (or anywhere else in the universe, for that matter), the individuals listed above are 100% responsible. Carry on.

(Signed)

Mother Nature